HOW TO SUCCEED AT
UNIVERSITY
(AND GET A GREAT JOB!)

On Campus

UBC Press is delighted to launch its *On Campus* imprint, featuring books, essays, and other materials designed to help students successfully tackle the intellectual and social challenges encountered at university or college today. *On Campus* will include a range of interesting, sometimes unconventional, perhaps humorous, but always useful information and advice for students to download for free or to purchase in print. In the past, such materials were only available informally, posted online by a professor for a class or photocopied and handed out manually year after year. The purpose of the *On Campus* imprint is to encourage wider availability of these underground sources of wisdom and to provide a hub where students can expect to find pertinent and accessible information on all kinds of topics related to university or college life. *On Campus* materials, while not peer-reviewed in the formal sense, do undergo a thorough assessment to ensure their suitability and value for their target audience.

The inaugural *On Campus* publication is *How to Succeed at University (and Get a Great Job!)*, written by York University professors Thomas R. Klassen and John A. Dwyer. Already a word-of-mouth phenomenon with steady sales in university bookstores, this revised edition will be an excellent resource for university students and graduates, college and high school students, as well as instructors, guidance counsellors, and parents. Lively, funny at times, and highly accessible, this practical guide argues that the best preparation for succeeding at life and on the job is succeeding at university. It is a prime example of the kinds of resources that UBC Press is proud to offer to the university community under the *On Campus* imprint.

THOMAS R. KLASSEN AND JOHN A. DWYER

HOW TO SUCCEED AT
UNIVERSITY
(AND GET A GREAT JOB!)

**MASTERING THE CRITICAL SKILLS YOU NEED
FOR SCHOOL, WORK, AND LIFE**

UBC PRESS

23 22 21 20 19 18 17 16   5 4 3 2

Printed in Canada on FSC-certified ancient-forest-free paper (100% post-consumer recycled) that is processed chlorine- and acid-free.

Library and Archives Canada Cataloguing in Publication

Klassen, Thomas R. (Thomas Richard), 1957-, author

How to succeed at university (and get a great job!): mastering the critical skills you need for school, work, and life / Thomas R. Klassen and John A. Dwyer.

Previously published under title: A practical guide to getting a great job after university, 2003.
Includes bibliographical references.
Issued in print and electronic formats.
ISBN 978-0-7748-3898-6 (pbk.). – ISBN 978-0-7748-3899-3 (pdf).

1. College students – Life skills guides. 2. Critical thinking. 3. Study skills. 4. Success. 5. Life skills. I. Dwyer, John, 1948-, author II.Title.

LB2343.3.K53 2015   378.1'98   C2015-901306-2
                                                        C2015-901307-0

Printed and bound in Canada by Friesens
Text design: Irma Rodriguez
Set in Huxley, Calibri, and Revival by Artegraphica Design Co. Ltd.
Copy editor: Deborah Kerr

UBC Press
The University of British Columbia
2029 West Mall
Vancouver, BC V6T 1Z2
www.ubcpress.ca

CONTENTS

PREFACE

We wrote this book to answer many of the questions that university students, and recent graduates, have about succeeding in their courses and in their post-school careers. All of our advice is a response to questions from the thousands of students we have taught at Ryerson University, Trent University, the University of British Columbia, Simon Fraser University, North Island College on Vancouver Island, and York University in Canada.

The book is the result of efforts by many people. Students and colleagues at York University urged us to write the first version, *A Practical Guide to a Great Job after University*. The encouraging responses from many readers – parents, academic advisors and guidance counsellors, and others, but most importantly students – enticed us to write an expanded second edition, *Flourishing in University and Beyond*.

Hundreds of students told us in e-mails, classrooms, and meetings that the book helped them find their way and sometimes changed their lives. York University and other universities have made it a required text for students who are beginning their post-secondary studies and a recommended text for those about to graduate. The book garnered positive reviews, including coverage in the *Globe and Mail* and other newspapers. That so many people benefitted from our advice and tips persuaded us to write a further revised and improved third edition. This you hold in your hands or see on your screen.

This edition includes new material on active listening, note taking, and managing social media, as well as updates of all the previous chapters. In writing this edition, we have been blessed to have the support of UBC Press. Emily Andrew, senior editor in Toronto, was an early champion of the book; without her assistance, the project would not have proceeded. In her quiet and effective manner, Melissa Pitts, director of UBC Press, ensured that all the elements of the book came together and fit perfectly. Holly Keller, manager of Production and Editorial Services, and her staff piloted the manuscript from ill-formed words to the lovely final product.

We remain grateful to former and current colleagues at York University – Stephen Glassman, Michael Jackel, and Michael Legris – who championed the earlier versions of the book. We are also deeply appreciative of our colleagues at the university and beyond who inspired us to write a work that integrates university studies and life skills, two sets of competencies that are too often separated.

In this edition, we continue to break down the barriers between the university experience and post-graduation careers. We steadfastly believe that the skills for academic and employment success are similar and that they can be learned. We know that people who combine sound advice with motivation invariably flourish in school and beyond.

HOW TO SUCCEED AT
UNIVERSITY
(AND GET A GREAT JOB!)

CHAPTER 1
University as Preparation for a Great Job

The best time is always the present time, because it alone offers the opportunity for action.

— Georges Vanier

Obtaining a university education is more expensive than ever, and more competitive. Unlike in the past, finishing a degree is not an assurance of a job, much less a good job. The labour market is more cutthroat, desirable jobs are fewer, and employers have higher expectations. New graduates must compete for jobs, not only with each other but often with people in other regions and countries.

Although students know that university is important to get a great job, seeing the relationship between the two can be difficult. Many courses seem irrelevant or overly abstract, and professors appear to have little understanding or appreciation of the *real* world. Sure, Shakespeare, Marx, and Plato are important to them, but what about to future employers? Many bosses and older colleagues, particularly in smaller companies, may not have gone to university and probably don't appreciate the hard work involved in getting a degree. As a result, it's easy to become cynical or depressed about attending classes, completing library research, assignments, and presentations, and writing exams.

By the time you finish your degree, you'll have paid a lot of money for that little piece of paper. For full-time undergraduates, the average cost of tuition alone is $6,000.[1] The cost of books, materials, and transportation will add considerably to this, as will accommodation for students who don't live at home. In total, a

BA or BSc will cost you at least $30,000 and possibly more if you need to re-take courses or decide to change programs. Some programs, such as business and computer science, will set you back an additional several thousand dollars in tuition each year. If you leave home to attend university, the total price tag for an undergraduate degree could be $70,000.

When you graduate, you will join the 25 percent of Canadian adults who have completed a university education. You will have worked hard and made many sacrifices – perhaps supported by your family – to join this group. But a degree is no guarantee that you will find a promising career.

To fully enjoy the fruits of your efforts, you would like convocation to be followed by a great job. The good news is that, if you play your cards right, it can and will be. This implies being smart and strategic about preparing for the job market and translating the skills you've learned at university into something sought-after!

Whether you're starting post-secondary studies or are in the middle or about to graduate, this book will help you learn the skills to succeed at school and in the challenging job market. It's meant for all university students, many college and high school students, and their parents. It should be read and applied from the time you begin your university career. But it offers a lot for anyone who is about to leave university for full-time permanent employment.

This book will also help you *flourish* as a student, a professional, and a person. Flourishing involves maximizing both your self-development and your contribution to others, including employers. Ultimately, it's about the happiness that comes when you live a thoughtful, balanced, and self-directed life. Don't be misled by these high-sounding words, however. There is nothing impractical about flourishing.

Many individuals don't flourish either at university or in the workplace because they obsess about getting a great job with a big paycheque. They respond uncritically to pressures from parents, friends, and others. Students are constantly bombarded with subtle but powerful messages about getting into one of the elite professions – such as law, medicine, and accounting – or taking specific courses and programs that have a *payoff*.

Your university experience and life will be diminished if you give in to this kind of tunnel vision. A university education can and does lead to financially rewarding and fulfilling employment. But job preparation is not its main purpose.

Attempting to address that task would be hopeless in any case. No one can accurately predict what the job market will be like after the four years that are usually required to get a degree. It makes more sense to enjoy your university experience rather than constantly worrying about your future. At the same time, it is good common sense to use your school years to help you succeed in life after your degree. You will flourish much better in university, work, and life if you pay attention to this dynamic relationship.

Not understanding how school relates to work, and work to school, means that you're not fully taking advantage of university studies to prepare yourself for the labour market. You don't need to be totally consumed with getting a job; in fact, we'll show how an obsession with gainful employment will probably backfire. But at the very least, you should be considering the connection between school and work.

The better you understand this link, the more prepared and the less stressed you will be about your future. And you'll have much more fun at university as well!

What's university all about?

"Toto, I've a feeling we're not in Kansas anymore." The classic line from *The Wizard of Oz* sums up the experience of many new university students. The standards are higher and the competition for good grades is tougher. And to top it off, the social and cultural transition from high school to university makes everything more difficult.

University is about preparing for the rest of your life, not just your job. You'll discover new and unimagined subjects that interest you. University involves many things: learning, meeting new people, making decisions, building new relationships, perhaps leaving home, travelling, dealing with money problems, working part-time and sometimes even full-time, and more.

You'll make new friends and might even meet a life partner. You will definitely learn lots about love, life, and your chosen field of study, but much of it will not seem applicable to your job and career after graduation. However, your time in school could – and should – be spent preparing for life in the workforce.

As we explain in this book, there is nothing better than university as a training ground for career ambitions. The bonus is that you can enjoy your university years as much as you like, while still making sure that you're ready to land the job of your dreams after graduation. Does this sound too good to be true? Read on.

What to expect after graduation

One of the greatest uncertainties about being in university is what will happen afterward – Will I find a good job? Will I like it? Will it pay enough? Will I need to move to find work? Will I get stuck in a rat race? Could I end up unemployed? These are crucial questions. Fortunately, many can be answered right now.

When you graduate, you will enter a professional workplace that is different from the one that your parents experienced, or are familiar with, if they attended post-secondary studies. Not so very long ago, a university degree was the ticket to a good and permanent position. However, organizations today require more than a degree – they are seeking a flexible problem solver who is good at multi-tasking, adapts well to change, and is a team player.

Your parents won't necessarily understand the pressure that you experience, since they might not have confronted the *same kind* of pressure. They want you to get a stable position and become self-sufficient as quickly as possible. Like your professors, they have a tendency to assume that not much has changed since they were young. Sometimes it helps to remind them what they were doing at your age.

But to become truly self-sufficient, and triumph, you must be much more proactive and flexible than they were at your age. Your career trajectory will be tough. This doesn't automatically mean that it will be stressful, and it certainly doesn't mean that it will be less interesting. It does mean, however, that you can't afford to be passive. You need to be strategic, creative, and opportunistic.

After four years of studying hard and living on peanuts, hoping to be rewarded with a stable and permanent job right after graduation is perfectly normal. This is unlikely to happen, however, because it's not how employers hire. Most employers hire recent university graduates on short-term contracts. This is a chance for both parties to test drive each other. Is there a good fit? Is the new employee willing and able to learn?

Today's public- and private-sector employers are not looking for someone who will stay with the organization permanently. They expect professional people to seek new opportunities every five years or so, and they realize that a significant percentage of present employees will be moving on, looking for other challenges and higher pay. Staying too long in one place can even be interpreted negatively – as lack of ambition! That's the reality of the work world that you will be entering.

Professionals need to be lifelong learners, continually updating or developing new skills as these are needed. Learning is being transformed from a stage in the life cycle into a continuous process. Individuals are responsible for seeking out the information and educational opportunities to keep abreast of their field or career trajectory. Those who are passive or reactive are left behind.

Given the importance of learning in your future professional life, it only makes sense to learn while at university. Most university courses are an ideal training ground for skills that will allow you to adapt in the workplace and beyond. After all, you will have a career to manage! Your university years offer a unique time to learn, practise, and perfect the skills that are essential for success in the workplace.

As a future professional, you will need four sets of skills:

▸ excellent communication (reading, writing, speaking, listening)
▸ the ability to learn and solve problems (in other words, the capacity for critical and creative "value-added" thinking)
▸ teamwork, including social skills (ethics, positive attitude, responsibility)
▸ a willingness to adapt to changing circumstances and to transfer knowledge to new situations.

The more of these skills you can acquire, the better prepared you will be to contribute to your profession and to fulfill your career goals. Guess what? These skills (no more and no less) are the key to success in university as well. This book is all about these skills.

Will I get a well-paid job?

Great jobs usually come with good salaries, and the majority of university graduates end up in well-paying positions. You want to join their ranks and guard against getting stuck in poorly paid and unfulfilling work.

Money doesn't guarantee happiness, but it sure as hell doesn't hurt either. A good income is a necessity since many graduates begin their first jobs mired in debt. Paying back your loan(s) and perhaps having money to travel, buy some of the things you've been deprived of, and maybe even get married are good incentives to take career preparation and the job search seriously.

The good news is that three years after completing a bachelor's degree, you will probably be earning about $53,000.[2] This is an average figure, of course. Some graduates will make considerably more and others less. The trick is to be among those who earn more and who, equally importantly, enjoy what they do!

How to select courses

One of the most stressful aspects of attending university is deciding on a program, major, or specialization, and courses. Sure, you get advice from guidance teachers, university counsellors, professors, family, and friends, but the decision is ultimately yours to make. And it's a *big* decision. Of course, some programs or courses may be off-limits because of various requirements and prerequisites. But there are still tons of choices to be made. Here is the best piece of advice in this book. Make these choices on your own terms, not somebody else's!

Trust yourself. Select programs and courses that interest you, without worrying too much *initially* about getting a job after graduation or earning a good salary. Yes, without considering the labour market! This is the most sensible approach because, ultimately, you need to find satisfaction in your courses, just as you will need to obtain satisfaction from your work after graduation.

For example, there's no sense in taking accounting only to fail your courses because you have zero interest in balance sheets and annual reports. Many students enrol in business-related programs and courses because they or their parents believe that doing so will result in a great job. The business curriculum is difficult and inflexible. After four or more years, some of these students would rather do anything else than work in business. What a waste of four years!

Wouldn't it be preferable to complete a degree in a subject that you like and in which you want to excel? After that, you can always do an MBA (master's degree in business administration), full-time or part-time, if you are still interested in the business route. Our point is that there's no need to make yourself miserable; you have choices. They should be *your* choices!

As you will read later in this book, a great job can be reached via many, many paths. Your path must be the one that is most enticing to you. Don't make the horrendous mistake of assuming that future success will be gained only through a painful process.

Picking courses that appeal to you is the best guarantee that you will succeed in them, and doing well (not necessarily achieving straight A's) is essential to getting a great job. A smooth road to a desirable job doesn't require being frustrated and unhappy, failing courses that you dislike, or constantly changing your major or program. This is a pointlessly expensive and *painful* way of attaining an education.

Mature, returning, and part-time students

For a number of reasons, including burnout (almost everyone experiences this at some point), you may decide to study part-time or return to university as a mature student. One of the really neat things about universities is that they are always there for you, which means that you can choose how and when to organize your learning.

Not everyone can or should be a full-time student. Part-time programs are available in most fields of study. Although some programs don't accept part-time students, this should not necessarily discourage you, as there may be creative ways to achieve what you want. On-line courses and programs are increasingly available, and they are accessible from anywhere at any time.

Studying part-time can be a good strategy, perhaps just for a summer or for a year, or for your entire degree. Part-time schooling also reinforces one of the most important truths about the world of work – learning does not stop at a predetermined age. The days when post-secondary education started in the late teens, was confined to a few years at university or college, and ended in the early twenties are vanishing. Don't get hung up on an outdated model.

If you cannot attend a post-secondary institution as soon as you graduate from high school, that's okay. In fact, having several years of *not* being in school can be an advantage when you apply to a university program.

To tell the truth, professors (including the ones who wrote this book) usually like students who have taken a break from school. These students are highly motivated, have better developed listening skills, and already know that success involves taking courses that appeal to them.

Returning students can face particular issues in relating school to their workforce experience, and vice versa. Sometimes they become too instrumental – that is, so concerned about how their education relates to the job market that they forget the joy of learning. In Chapter 11, we cover some matters related to returning to school after being in the workforce for a while.

What job-related skills can I learn in my courses?

Nearly all the skills that you will learn and use in your courses are exactly what you'll need for an interesting, challenging, and well-paying job. Surprised?

Doing oral presentations, working in groups, meeting deadlines, overcoming challenges, looking at problems from differing perspectives, concisely summarizing information, identifying links and patterns, locating and sifting sources of information, explaining past events and projecting what may occur in the future, writing well and with some analytical depth, and dealing with people in positions of authority are almost certainly part of your ideal job. These are the skills that you can, and must, develop at university.

Consider any professional occupation or any senior position in the private or public sector. People who hold these jobs spend hours each day communicating with others: convincing them of new ideas and proposals, obtaining and understanding information, explaining matters in person or in writing. They also devote considerable time and effort to looking at events and circumstances in a critical and creative manner to solve problems and make improvements: Why did we have a financial loss this quarter? How could we develop a stronger and timelier strategy? Why did some of my students fail? Why were the ethics of our organization breached? How does what happened today relate to what happened last month and might happen tomorrow? Finally, anyone who wants to be a professional must be able to work well with others, including supervisors, colleagues, subordinates, clients, and stakeholders.

One of the authors of this book worked for a year as the placement director for a prestigious MBA school, where students were recruited by leading Canadian and global corporations. What all these well-known companies wanted in potential employees – even more than high grades – was the ability to solve problems creatively, communicate effectively, work as part of a team, and adapt to changes.

When the recruiters for blue-chip companies studied resumes or interviewed candidates, they looked for evidence that these *universal* skills had been learned. They expertly and ruthlessly sifted out those who merely had good memories, thought *inside the box*, lacked people skills, or were inflexible.

Although higher education is one of the best investments a person can make, it is *not* a guarantee of a good and fulfilling position. You need to use your years in university to acquire, and practise, the all-important four sets of skills:

▸ communication
▸ problem solving
▸ teamwork
▸ adaptability.

The amazing thing is that by doing so, you will succeed wonderfully in your courses and will also find the time to enjoy all the other benefits that a university education provides.

The following chapters give you hints and advice on how to acquire – in your courses – the skills that guarantee success at school and work. Chapter 2 looks in more depth at the general skills that you can, and must, acquire at university to ensure your success as a professional. Chapter 3 explains how to use the exams, essays, and reports that you write for your courses to prepare for your first job and career. Chapter 4 reveals how to acquire the critical skills that are essential to success in university. Chapters 5 and 6 help you to become an active listener and reader, and to strengthen research skills. Chapters 7 and 8 consider the problem-solving skills that are required to deal with university, the office, and life situations more generally. Chapter 9 shows the nuts and bolts of the post-university job search. Social media, and using them to your advantage, are the focus of Chapter 10. And Chapter 11 closes the book by looking at the workplace and beyond.

One final point before proceeding. The skills that are effective and result in success in university and the labour market may be virtually identical, but they do need to be adapted or rejigged to suit their particular context. The skill set may be the same, but the time frame, expectations, and environment will be different.

Nobody ever claimed that university was the *real world*. However, the path from university to the real world is straightforward and exciting if you know what you are doing.

CHAPTER 2
Skills for Success at School and Work

There is only one thing more painful than learning from
experience and that is not learning from experience.

— Archibald MacLeish

As we mentioned in the last chapter, all professionals need to be
good at communicating, solving problems, working as part of a
team, and adapting to change. Without mastering at least one of
these areas, you can probably kiss your career prospects goodbye.
However, communicating well is perhaps the most important of
the four. After all, can a lawyer, social worker, teacher, business
executive, manager, entrepreneur, journalist, or any other professional achieve success without first-rate communication skills?

This chapter explains how some of the most neglected, and
disliked, aspects of university courses will be invaluable in your
later activities. Our experience, and that of many recent graduates, is irrefutable: giving presentations, performing group work,
becoming proactive, taking notes, and getting yourself organized
will not only make your life easier at school, but will also help in
your post-graduation job. Let's begin with oral presentations.

Oral presentations

For many students, giving a presentation in a class or tutorial is one
of the worst parts of the university experience. The symptoms
of presentation flu include sweaty palms, stomach butterflies, and

total paralysis. Presentations are stressful, preparing them is time consuming, and you never quite know what to expect. Yet, they are among the most job-related activities that university has to offer.

We prefer to use a broad definition of oral presentations. At the formal end of the scale, you may have to stand in front of a class and speak on a topic of your instructor's or your own choosing. But this type of presentation differs in intensity rather than in kind from many more casual interactions in the classroom. All of them are important for success at school.

This is equally true in the world of work. Without good presentation skills, you will have great difficulty even landing a job. After all, your first oral presentation for your employer will be your interview! Since today's jobs rarely translate to employment for life, you will have to endure many of these intense ordeals if you want to advance your career or even keep working.

Chances are that presentations will play a major role in your life as a professional. Whether delivered formally to a large audience or given casually at a breakfast or lunch meeting, they are a common way of sharing information in the professional world. If you become a manager or owner of a business, much of your day will involve preparing, delivering, and reacting to presentations of one kind or another. And unless your employer locks you in the basement, you'll give many presentations as part of your job. You will be responsible for explaining something, communicating your ideas to others, and encouraging the people with whom you interact. Your audiences will include customers, clients, investors, colleagues, supervisors, and perhaps the general public. Even if you don't give many presentations in your first job, you'll probably prepare them for your supervisor. In any case, your boss and your co-workers will not be impressed if your abilities in this area are poor.

Because presentations are so crucial in the world of work, many a promising career has been sabotaged by the inability to communicate well. So why not learn to do it now, when the stakes are not nearly as high? Use your university years to practise. If a course requires a formal presentation, try to schedule it early in the term, when there are fewer conflicts with tests and other assignments. Also, learn how to use PowerPoint or other presentation software. Your employer, colleagues, and clients will expect you to use such software and associated technology. In this situation, the time and effort invested in school presentations will pay off handsomely.

If your courses do not include formal presentations, they nonetheless provide many opportunities to develop your verbal skills. Asking questions of your professor or tutorial/lab assistant is a type of oral presentation in miniature. Even talking to instructors during office hours or in other situations is a form of presentation, for which you should prepare if you want to be effective.

Giving a class presentation is stressful, but if you follow the steps below, it will become less so. You might even begin to enjoy it!

Don't forget our first and best piece of advice in this book. Presentations are so much easier if the topic interests you. After all, why speak on something that bores you to tears? Thus, the key is to take courses (and ultimately be in a career) that satisfy you.

Even if you're stuck with a bad presentation topic – perhaps because others snagged all the good ones, or the professor assigned it to you – don't settle for mediocrity. Only an uncreative person can't find something of interest in an unappealing subject. Would you hire a person like that? At some point during your career, you will work on, and talk about, material that does not interest you. Practising in school can give you the skills to do this well.

This leads us to the overwhelming key to success as a presenter: enthusiasm! Nothing is more contagious, effective, or compelling. The best teachers and the best presenters are those who convey personal enthusiasm and passion. When this is combined with knowledge and a little practice, the final result is always awesome.

All this work for one short presentation may seem like a lot of time and effort. But it is not really, partly because the more you prepare and rehearse, the easier the next presentation will be. You may feel that you have too little time to get ready, but that's life. Once you're employed full-time in a responsible position, you'll have far less time to prepare. Your boss, clients, and colleagues will expect you to hit the ground running. In asking you to speak on a topic, your supervisor may give you short notice, or no notice at all. Why not take advantage of your university years to get good at it?

Think some people are just better at verbal communication than others? The truth is that anyone can significantly improve this skill. One of the authors of this book has a disability that most of you don't share. He stutters, and as a high school and university student, he never once raised his hand or answered a question. Nonetheless, he's learned to become a highly effective teacher, lecturer, and communicator.

When you are good at something difficult, it becomes satisfying and even pleasurable. Giving presentations is obviously difficult, so delivering an effective one can be amazing. Just check out the faces of your classmates following a successful presentation.

Treat presentations as an opportunity to develop a useful skill, to demonstrate your ability to simplify material, and to really impress your instructors and classmates (and more importantly, yourself). Here are easy-to-use tips for formal presentations that you can adapt to your own situation:

▹ Be proactive. Always think of a presentation as a chance to impress everyone, not just with how hard you've worked, but also with how clever and original you've been.

▹ Stage a dress rehearsal. Practice makes perfect. Practise in front of the mirror or your siblings, friends, or others. Video or audiotape yourself. This is a useful exercise for everything from lengthy presentations to asking a question in tomorrow's class.

▹ Appearance is half the battle. Dress well to show everyone how serious you are about your talk and how much you respect your audience.

▹ Arrive early. Check all your equipment. Go over your notes. Decide how you intend to greet people.

▹ Provide a warm welcome. Get your audience on your side right away. Introduce both yourself and your topic. Remember that your listeners want you to succeed.

▹ Smile a lot, but don't joke around. One bad joke can kill you.

▹ Appear confident and composed, even if your stomach is full of butterflies.

▹ Talk directly to your audience. Never read from notes if you can help it, and don't over-prepare so as to become mechanical. Refer to your notes only if you get stuck.

▷ Aim to be yourself, but watch the mannerisms. Everyone has nervous tics. Identify, eliminate, or transform them into useful gestures by practising in a mirror or taping yourself.

▷ Vary the activities. Remember that listeners have a short attention span.

▷ Present the audience with a clear summary that can be useful as a study guide for an exam. Your fellow students will enjoy your presentation that much more if it also saves them some work.

▷ Always try to have at least one surprise up your sleeve. If you can provide extra value that no one expected, your presentation will be memorable. If appropriate, bring candy or other goodies to distribute. Be creative in this.

▷ Finish on a strong note and don't be overly modest. False modesty is for losers. Winners try to leave with a bang.

▷ No one enjoys criticism, but try to see it as constructive, and don't be defensive if questions are asked after your talk. Respond briefly and positively, with something like, "You make a really good point, thank you."

You may think that oral presentations are overrated, but consider why professors and employers choose them rather than other modes of conveying information or ideas:

▷ Presentations are the most personalized delivery of material. Think of how powerful they are at persuading an audience to buy a product or accept an idea.

▷ Half of all interpersonal communication takes the form of facial expressions and body language.

▷ People learn better when they see and hear at the same time. A good presentation allows the audience to see and hear the speaker. The appropriate use of slides or other material helps the audience to internalize and remember the information.

▷ The printed page cannot easily display the rhetorical styles and devices that are available to a good speaker. He or she can pause for effect, adjust to feedback, change tone and emphasis, and invite and answer questions.

▷ A well-prepared and well-delivered presentation demonstrates a real commitment to the audience. By showing this level of respect for their listeners, speakers also earn far greater respect for their subject matter than is possible in any other format.

Inexperienced and poor presenters tend to make the same six mistakes.

1 *Not projecting clearly.* The greatest presentation in the world is useless if no one can hear it. Practise speaking in various places to ensure that everyone in the room hears you. Many presenters speak too quietly and have a tendency to mumble, especially when looking down at their notes. People who give an inaudible talk are simply demonstrating that they don't want to be there, that they don't know, and that they don't really care.

2 *Not making eye contact.* One advantage of a presentation is its potential for interaction and rapport with the audience. These cannot be achieved, however, unless the speaker makes eye contact with listeners. Again, the failure to do so is a sure sign of uncertainty and lack of engagement with either the material or the presentation.

3 *Giving too much information.* This is the worst mistake of inexperienced and insecure speakers, who often try to take on too much. A good rule of thumb is that an audience can absorb no more than three big ideas, each of which should be illustrated by two or three examples. If listeners are given more, they'll begin to tune out. Identify what absolutely must be conveyed and omit the rest. No presentation will communicate all, or even most, of what you know.

4 *Running over time.* How do you feel about instructors who keep talking after the class has ended? There is no better way to sabotage an otherwise good presentation than by going over time. Doing so tells your listeners that your time is more important than theirs, which completely defeats the atmosphere of mutual respect that you've been trying to create. If you suspect that you

won't finish on time, simply leave things out. Trust us, the audience won't notice.

To avoid running over time, give a talk that's shorter than its allotted period. This not only ensures that you will finish on time, but will also provide you with a few minutes to take questions at the end.

5 *Handing out material.* Make material available before or after your presentation. Distribute it during your talk *only* if you'll be completely going through it with your listeners. Otherwise, they'll stop focusing on you. Some will immediately begin to read it, and you'll need to work extra hard to regain their attention. It's much smarter not to lose it in the first place.

6 *Using audio-visual aids inappropriately.* Don't be seduced by technology! A successful presentation rarely depends on whiz-bang audio-visual effects, which can be a huge distraction if not used properly or if they don't work well. If you project slides on a screen, don't just read them – use them to guide or highlight your main themes. Ensure that visual aids are

- employed appropriately and in context
- used to enhance, rather than distract from, your points
- simple and easy to see or hear.

For many people, the most stressful part of a presentation is when the audience asks questions, especially the professor (or boss). But remember, you are in charge. Because you've done the necessary research and preparation, you're the expert on the topic. For anyone in the audience who has read or understood less than you – even your teacher – you are the expert! You control all the dynamics of the presentation, and you structure the framework for questions and answers.

Set the ground rules right away to favour your strengths. If you'd prefer not to answer questions until the end, say so at the beginning. On the other hand, if you want to maintain an interactive atmosphere, you can ask the audience to raise questions as your talk unfolds.

Encouraging listeners to ask questions is a good way of inviting them into a relationship with you. It's your invitation, rather than the questions themselves, that is most important in bonding with the audience.

Make your invitation genuine. Don't just say "Any questions?" and then immediately sit down. Give the audience a chance to interact with you. Say something along the lines of "I hope you have some questions for me" or "Is there anything that you'd like me to clarify or explore further?"

Maintain eye contact with the audience. Smile. Wait. Twenty seconds can seem like twenty minutes when you're waiting for someone to speak up, but people need time to shift from listening mode to questioning mode. Wait for this to happen.

Whenever you get a question, repeat it for the audience. This will demonstrate that you see it as important (and will gratify the questioner) and will also invite everyone in the room to share in it.

Rephrase negative questions, which are sometimes referred to as interjections or interventions, in a positive way. They usually signal that someone is trying to parade his or her intelligence at your expense. Don't try to shut that person down, since this negates your accessibility. Simply highlight the positive.

Never bluff or lose your composure. You're not expected to know everything. If you don't know, say so. But don't stop there. Add that you will be happy to get the information for anyone who is interested. If you are experienced in retaking control of the discussion, you can even throw the question out to the audience to see if anyone there has an answer. But don't try this unless you know how to get the attention back to you.

Politely end unproductive questions or discussions. You are in charge. The audience expects you to gently prevent people from rambling and to close off dead ends. Remind everyone why you are doing this by saying something like, "Can you complete your question, as I see that more people are waiting to speak?" or "I'm sure that there are lots of other issues that people want to raise; let's move on."

When someone asks a weak question, convert it into a good one, using it as an opportunity to demonstrate your skill and really win over your audience. Seasoned presenters are adept at finding a grain of brilliance in a bad question and turning it to their advantage. The inquirer will rarely challenge the interpretation, since the question has been reworked into something that puts him or her in a flattering light. The perceptive people in the audience will appreciate that an awkward situation has been handled without slighting the individual's dignity. It's a win-win situation for everyone.

Most notably, don't get defensive and try to justify yourself in response to questions. It's hard to hear "You've left this out" or "I don't agree" or even "You're wrong." The instinctive reaction is to launch into a lengthy explanation or repeat parts of your talk. Don't put yourself in this position. Instead, answer all questions briefly and don't hesitate to reply with "That's an excellent point you've made and something I will consider."

Always thank your listeners for asking questions, and tell them that they've been a good audience. If you make this point, they're bound to conclude that you're an effective presenter!

Hopefully, you will now begin to see oral presentations not so much as chores, but as something valuable, interesting, and even fun. We now discuss another activity that students often dislike but that is almost as vital for success in the workplace.

Group work

While you were in high school, you probably engaged in at least some group work. Under the direction of a good teacher, it can be exhilarating. But it's often the case that some group members work harder than others, though everyone gets the credit. In university, many students start to see group projects as a waste of precious time, one that does not recognize their individual effort.

Don't let negative experiences cloud your judgment about the value of group projects. In the world of work, people rarely operate in isolation. The success of companies and organizations is based on effective collaboration. And unlike in high school, if you don't contribute to the success of the group, your reputation will suffer and you won't last long.

Today's business community and employer marketplace are big on collaboration. Given this, it's not surprising that all presentations in business schools and many other professional university programs are given by teams. What's fascinating about group presentations is the way that individuals build on their own areas of expertise to come up with something much better than they would have achieved on their own.

Despite these advantages, teamwork does have its drawbacks. Almost always, there are differences about how to proceed; disagreements take time to resolve; and not everyone works equally hard.

However, you must learn to deal with these frustrations. In your future job, you will work primarily in groups. Writing a document (such as a proposal) on your own and submitting it to one person for review is rare in the workplace. Most activities are group-based. In fact, functioning well in a team setting will get you jobs, whereas the inability to do this will cost you jobs and promotions.

Group work is crucial because nearly every activity at any workplace involves complex undertakings that are beyond the skills of any one person. This means that you will be part of one or more teams in any job you have. Even if you are self-employed, you will work collaboratively with clients, suppliers, and many others.

Use your university years to hone your skills at collaborating with others. Try to join various types of groups: with males and females, older and younger students, international students, and those whose background differs from yours. Take on diverse roles: sometimes be a leader and sometimes a follower.

Observe how group members *interact*. Watch how others behave and react. Think about how the team could operate differently. See how gender, ethnic background, and other factors affect its functioning. Pay attention to the way in which the final product benefits from this diversity of experiences and viewpoints.

Collaborative presentations and projects pose distinct challenges. Here are easy-to-use tips that can be adapted to any group situation:

▶ Always engage in a group brainstorming session before deciding on a strategy. Don't let one person dictate the plan. Everyone needs to have ownership of the project.

▶ Ensure that everyone has a specific role to play in the project. But also make sure that everyone understands that this does not absolve him or her of responsibility for the project as a whole.

▶ If group pressure can't improve matters, be prepared to eject members who are dragging their feet. This may be difficult if you are a student, but the group can approach an instructor (and later on your boss!) for help in dealing with people who don't pull their weight.

▶ Act as a team during the presentation or project. If you have no role to play at a particular time, your job is either to support what your colleagues are doing or to reflect group solidarity with clients or audiences. Always be prepared to help your colleagues if they run into problems.

▶ Don't showboat. Some people have a tendency to take over leadership roles and dominate the group. This has a negative impact on the presentation or project as a whole.

▶ Achieve closure. Celebrate the project's completion with your colleagues. However briefly, you were an effective team and you want to show each other gratitude and respect.

As with oral presentations, we hope you might now see group work as an interesting and valuable activity. Look for opportunities to develop these skills.

The effectiveness of collaboration is something that every progressive employer understands. So, if you want to work for a "with it" company or organization, be prepared to abandon the temptation to fly solo.

The *real magic* of group work is that what you can achieve in partnership with others is a quantum leap over what you can achieve alone. The destination is well worth any frustration encountered along the way, and the time spent is well spent.

Being a proactive professional

Proactive individuals, sometimes referred to as *self-starters*, are in high demand at public and private organizations. The problem, according to university professors and employers, is that too many students and graduates are passive and expect to be spoon-fed by their instructors or supervisors. If you fall into this category, you're not ready for the real world.

In some ways, university courses don't differ much from the work that you'll probably do after graduation. Just like your professors and teaching assistants, your manager or client will give you vague instructions, expecting you to figure them out for yourself. If you want a job that comes with clear and detailed directions, it probably won't be the job of your dreams and certainly won't be the work of a professional.

A telling characteristic of "Mc" jobs is that they don't ask staff to think or be self-starters. That's why they pay so badly. If you want a good job, let go of the need to have someone lead you by the hand. Take the initiative yourself.

At school, demonstrate the professionalism that you intend to exhibit in the workforce. Submit your assignments on time, and don't be late for class. Read the syllabus carefully. Do your reading before class so that you can benefit from the instructor's interpretation. If you treat your classes casually, chances are that you'll treat your future job in just the same way.

That's the real reason why employers are interested in your grades. People who get good grades are conscientious, dedicated, and proactive about the specific tasks involved in attending university. An A implies being well prepared and going beyond what is expected.

Try to figure things out on your own, in a creative manner, rather than running to your teaching assistant or professor with every question. Your boss, clients, and colleagues will certainly not appreciate being bothered too often with relatively unimportant questions or requests for reassurance.

Asking for a deadline extension on the day that an assignment is due may be acceptable in some courses, but this approach will certainly limit your post-graduate career. Having a breakdown in front of your professor because of stress, lack of sleep, or poor diet the day before the final exam may win you sympathy at university. A similar collapse in front of your boss or client will cost you a promotion, if not your job.

A piece of helpful advice is to avoid getting fixated on grades when you speak with a professor. Feel free to ask how you might better understand material or improve your performance. After all, grades are just a reflection of your comprehension and knowledge.

In the same manner, your boss or clients will react quite poorly to discussions about your pay or how pleased they are with your work, but will be far more interested in discussing the content of the work you have done.

There will be times when you need something from a professor or teaching assistant. Again, approach this situation like a professional – prepare your evidence or question, rehearse, and try to analyze the situation. Professors are professionals and teaching assistants are professionals in training. They have many duties to perform in addition to teaching and a perfect right to object whenever anyone wastes their time.

You may believe that university and work are so different that you can be late with school assignments, write your papers the night before the deadline, cram for exams, miss classes, do the minimum, and be disorganized, but that as soon as you graduate you will become a different person. In a few rare cases this is true, but the way you handle your years in university is a good predictor of what you'll be like after graduation. Certainly, potential employers have this view, based on many years of hiring university graduates.

Of course, in some important aspects, the classroom is not like the office. In class, you have much more freedom to speak your mind and can explore issues of personal interest to a much greater degree than most workplaces will ever allow. If you choose to cut classes or not to participate in classroom discussions, there are few repercussions, other than not learning much (after all, you are paying for your education). Nevertheless, the degree of professionalism that you display in university remains the single best indicator of your performance after graduation.

Other valuable skills can be learned at school. It is true that many of them can be acquired in other ways, such as from travelling or part-time work. But university has an advantage when it comes to gaining or strengthening these skills – it was created specifically to facilitate learning.

For example, universities are serious about embracing cultural diversity because doing so reflects breadth of mind and an appreciation for knowledge from a variety of sources. University is not the only place to learn about other cultures, but most of your teachers will be willing to help you explore cultural differences. And it's a lot easier to learn about others when they are your peers, engaged in a safe laboratory designed to promote learning.

Information about other cultures is invaluable in any profession that hopes to succeed in our global economy. Did you know that among Asians, only Koreans use the family name of "Park," and that 25 percent of all Koreans have it as their surname? So, when you're in your great job and you meet an Asian client or customer with that name, you'll be a step ahead.

Deep knowledge of other cultures can be very useful. North American organizations can learn a lot from their Asian counterparts. Japanese and South Korean corporations are successful partly because they focus on group dynamics as much as individual achievement and because they have a long-term perspective.

At university, you are encouraged to systematically explore connections such as those between culture and business. It would be much more difficult, and haphazard, to learn such things on the job. And you probably don't want to ask a new client to explain some aspect of her culture or family.

In fact, since it is almost guaranteed that you'll be dealing with clients, customers, colleagues, and bosses from other cultures, why not get a step ahead at university? Are some of your classmates from other cultures and other parts of the world? Why not learn from them? The benefits of a university education are multiplied when formal and informal learning is integrated in a systematic way.

So why not consider being systematic about it? Memorize a few phrases from other languages. Learn the appropriate way of greeting people (bow, shake hands, one kiss on the cheek, two kisses). Learn about different kinds of people from diverse backgrounds. Explore other cultures (and perspectives) more deeply.

Don't ever presume that your ethnic community or socio-economic group has all the answers. A more broad-based and in-depth knowledge will make you a better professional in whatever field you enter, from business, to science, to social work.

An important fact to consider is that some of your classmates may ultimately become your clients, colleagues, or customers. Entrepreneurs and senior executives often appoint their university roommates and friends to top positions. Managers who are looking for new employees often consult with their acquaintances for contacts. Informal networking and word of mouth are much more important than formal job applications. Whom you know may not be as important as what you know, but knowing how to make someone part of your network is crucial. (For more on networking, see Chapter 9.)

Some general skills, though not taught in classrooms, dovetail nicely with university education. For example, universities provide encouragement and opportunities for students who want to gain new skills, such as writing, researching, and mastering computer technology. The off-campus equivalents of the mini-courses and workshops offered at university come with a hefty price tag.

Technology changes constantly, but don't hide your head in the sand. Try to keep abreast of developments. Using a basic word processing program is no longer an advantage in getting a job. Many employers want staff who, at the very least, can use spreadsheets such as Excel, graphic and display software, and Internet-based tools. If your courses don't include this information, take advantage of free campus workshops, usually offered through the library or the writing centre, which will help you develop these skills.

Finally, a university, particularly a large one, is also a place of work and opportunity. A variety of jobs are available at school, and they can provide valuable experience. Some are voluntary, but many are paid. There are numerous work-study positions, and professors often hire students part-time to conduct research, interview groups, and help run computer labs. In addition, there are dozens of clubs, sports teams, associations, radio stations, and theatre groups that often need staff.

When they hire recent graduates, many corporations check their resume for evidence of involvement in clubs or athletics. Why? Because many potential employers are impressed by someone who can combine academics with extracurricular activities; it demonstrates balance, commitment, a willingness to work hard, and teamwork.

And let's not forget the obvious – joining a campus or residence group or organization that holds some interest for you will bring you much pleasure and satisfaction.

We trust that you're beginning to get our message. The university is an ideal environment for developing job-related skills. Even if your courses don't offer you many chances for group work and oral presentations, you can find them elsewhere on campus. Have you begun to realize some of the ways you can make opportunities for yourself?

You may be thinking that university sounds like a lot of work: classes and everything that goes with them, extracurricular and volunteer activities, and possibly part-time employment. And it is, if you're serious about finding a great job after graduation. The good news, though, is that if you take courses that you like and participate in activities that you enjoy, it won't seem like work at all. It will be fun, as will your future career.

Using numbers

Not all of our advice is going to sound like fun. Here comes the hard part.

Increasingly, employers need workers who are proficient with numbers. In other words, they should be numerate. More and more, to be a professional means to manipulate and understand numerical information. More generally, all citizens need a basic understanding of math to make informed decisions about investments, loans, and banking, and to make sense of the world.

Some of your courses will enable you to do this, especially the ones with lab work. Some programs of study provide fewer opportunities, but there are always options to strengthen your comfort level in dealing with numbers.

Typically, many social science and humanities students avoid enrolling in courses that involve a lot of numbers. This decision is reasonable since quantitative courses (such as statistics and research methods) are demanding and intimidating.

The good news is that such courses are actually difficult to fail (almost all students who persevere to the end will pass) and do provide useful skills in the labour force and other parts of life. Being able to tell a potential employer during an interview that you have basic quantitative or research skills will always work in your favour.

You don't necessarily have to enrol in a course to improve your proficiency with figures. Consider learning to use Excel or a similar spreadsheet program; lessons are often given free on campus, and many Excel tutorials are also available on YouTube. Or get a friend or classmate to help you. People just love to show how numerate they are!

Using spreadsheet software or even more advanced programs such as SPSS (Statistical Package for the Social Sciences), SAS, and other data analysis tools is not as painful as supposed by even the most mathematically challenged. The key for many people is to structure their learning around a specific problem or task. Try plotting your grades. Can you do that? Can you quickly calculate an average, using Excel or similar software? Can you plot how much money you will need to invest?

Many term papers and assignments benefit from the inclusion of a table or chart. Check your textbooks to see how they use charts and tables to quickly illustrate a point, rather than explaining it in additional paragraphs. Consider applying the same strategy. You wouldn't believe how impressed your professor will be, especially if he or she is not particularly numerate.

There is such a mystique about numbers that any level of expertise has a payoff. Learning these skills can be rewarding (dare we say fun?). A graph, chart, or table often increases the grade of an essay or assignment. And without a doubt, the ability to create a simple chart, graph, or spreadsheet helps determine who is hired for a position and who is rejected. You can be certain that at the very least, many of your bosses, colleagues, and clients will expect you to be confident with numbers.

Being somewhat numerate may have the biggest payoff in your future career. It's no accident that many CEOs and senior managers of large corporations once studied accounting and business, often after they completed an undergraduate degree in the social sciences or humanities.

Taking notes

You may think that taking notes in class, and from textbooks, is unique to university. In fact, quite the opposite! Taking good notes is integral to just about any professional occupation that you can name.

For example, social workers, police officers, bankers, health care professionals, and lawyers must take very detailed notes concerning clients and events. Their notes may become critical pieces of evidence in courts of law, often years after they were written. Teachers keep notes on the progress of students, which are later summarized in the form of report cards. Journalists and other writers depend on their skills in taking notes. Financial advisors make notes of the preferences and investment advice of their clients and must be able to recall this information quickly.

At any important meeting in business and government, someone will take notes. For your first few years in the labour force, you may be required to prepare the minutes of various meetings. One of the authors of this book began his administrative career by taking notes at meetings for a vice-president of a large organization.

You can be assured that many times during your career, you will be asked to "Attend tomorrow's meeting for me and take notes so that I'll know what happened" or to "Read over this report and write me a summary." Doing this well will get you noticed and rewarded. Doing it poorly will only get you noticed.

The office of any professional will contain drawers, or computer folders, of notes taken at professional development courses, observations on the performance of subordinates, remarks on work to be done, various letters and related documents, and status reports about ongoing projects and activities.

The keys to creating good notes in the professional world are exactly the same as at university – clarity, conciseness, and precision. But writing notes at school is easier because no one else will read them, whereas in the workforce other people will often use your notes.

When taking notes at a lecture or meeting, aim to

▹ summarize complex information succinctly
▹ organize material in a meaningful way (the lecture or meeting may have been unfocused, but your notes should be the opposite)

▷ highlight the key ideas and clarify their significance
▷ incorporate and subordinate facts and concepts within themes or big ideas
▷ include the insights from various sources (the speaker, readings, questions asked, past events)
▷ pinpoint areas and problems that require further exploration.

Some telltale signs of ineffective note taking, in university and elsewhere, are

▷ furiously trying to record everything (there is no excuse for this, because notes are a summary)
▷ lack of eye contact with the speaker (continue to engage with him or her even as you write)
▷ absence of questions or matters that need further illumination (if possible, ask questions of the speaker to help clarify matters)
▷ notes that are either disjointed or organized in only point form (these are no help to anyone).

Techniques that can develop your skill as a note taker in university include

▷ always reading the materials that relate to the lecture beforehand
▷ creating your own shorthand to remind you of important connections or questions (such as =, ?, >>, N.B.); N.B. stands for *nota bene*, or note well!
▷ re-reading your notes while they are still fresh and making any connections or embellishments that you could not develop during the lecture
▷ answering any questions that you posed in your notes, either by consulting the readings, other students, or your teacher
▷ regularly summarizing all your notes on a particular course unit or section
▷ comparing your notes with those of other students in your study group.

The authors have lots of experience in teaching university students in large lectures. We can tell you with some authority that the ability to take good notes makes a major difference between students who do well in their coursework and those who struggle.

Many students use a computer to take notes, and some classes even require them to do this. Our strong recommendation is to use pen and paper. This is because taking notes with a computer or tablet is a temptation to multi-task – to search for information on-line, to play games, watch movies, or even visit the social network.

Multi-tasking during lectures, no matter how appealing, reduces grades. Don't believe us? Check the studies that compared students who handwrote their notes to those who used laptops. Students who relied on laptops scored 17 percent lower on tests; that translates to dropping from a B+ to a B.[3]

Taking good notes, and earning good grades, is best done sitting in the middle or near the front of a classroom, with smartphone and computer turned off. Choosing a seat in the back row is not conducive to learning, and a smartphone distracts from an activity that requires your full attention. Make a habit of sitting close to the front, and you will quickly find that listening and taking notes are easier and more fulfilling.

If you don't learn to take good notes at university, be assured that acquiring this skill later on will be much more painful and career limiting.

Getting yourself organized

One of the biggest initial difficulties in completing tasks at school or work is motivation. This, again, reinforces a central theme of this book – that you must select courses and jobs that appeal to you. However, even if you've done this, sitting down and doing the work can sometimes be difficult.

We all procrastinate at some point, getting distracted or twiddling our thumbs instead of learning. If you believe that writing this book was easy for us because we are professors and are deeply committed to the material, think again!

Below are some suggestions that have helped us and will help you get going during those times when you'd prefer not to work. These apply equally to school and the job.

SET YOURSELF GOALS AND SUB-GOALS

Just as you need reasons and goals to get fit or learn a sport, you need to motivate yourself to start a university project, whether it's studying for a test, writing a paper, or tackling something else. Your overarching goals can be as abstract as becoming a good speaker, making a contribution to society, or meeting the reasonable expectations of your parents or others.

Your sub-goals should be specific enough to provide you with the rewards that will keep you motivated. Many students use their career as a goal and good grades as a sub-goal. There's nothing wrong with that, as long as you realize that good grades also need to be divided into many sub-goals.

Getting good grades typically involves

- studying the materials carefully
- completing all the necessary and recommended assignments
- attending all the lectures and taking good notes
- working in groups with other students, or at least reviewing your notes and reading assignments with others
- being proactive by doing that extra bit of reading, research, and writing.

If you meet these sub-goals, reward yourself on a regular basis. You've earned it! By breaking down goals into sub-goals, you will avoid the question that paralyzes many students and leads to procrastination – "I've got so much to do; what should I do first?"

MANAGE YOUR TIME

Students often do things at the last minute, not because they're lazy, but because it's a quick and dirty method of organizing and motivating themselves. The eighteenth-century writer and inventor of the dictionary, Samuel Johnson (1709-84), once remarked that a person could really get focused on the night before his execution. Some students seem to share this view, and some will even claim that they do their best work on the night before the deadline.

Teachers and experienced students know that this is not true, as do successful professionals. Would you like to be operated on by an overly stressed and exhausted surgeon who does her work while mainlining coffee? Do you want to be represented by a lawyer who didn't sleep on the night before your court date and cannot focus?

Some people are better than others at managing their time. Perhaps their brains are wired differently, or perhaps they absorbed good time management skills from their parents or significant others. But most of us need to plan our time and stick to a schedule. Time is the most precious commodity that a busy university student has; that's why using it well is so important.

Here are tips to avoid wasting time:

▸ Make yourself follow a routine. Try to get up at the same time each morning and go to bed at the same time each night. According to planning experts, establishing a daily routine is the best way to leverage time spent on tasks and maximize accomplishments.

▸ Create a schedule for your academic term that includes all due dates for assignments and exams.

▸ Calculate backward from the due date for each assignment or exam to determine when you should begin working and how many hours you need to invest to be successful in the activity. Most courses, to the frustration of students, are back-end-loaded. In other words, the bulk of the work is required late in the term. Minimize this "crunch time" by planning and working far in advance of deadlines.

▸ Identify priorities. Some subjects or assignments are more important than others. Spending a lot of time on an unimportant task is a common mistake of inexperienced students and professionals. You can highlight major priorities by using different fonts or inks of various colours. Always be prepared to adjust priorities as the term progresses.

▸ Use assignment and weekly planners (see examples on page 36). At the end of each week or month, spend an hour in reviewing these planners so that you can make any necessary adjustments.

▸ Aim for steady improvement rather than perfection. This advice is especially important for students who are just beginning to develop a particular skill. You're bound to be lousy at something when you try it for the first time. That's life. What's important is getting better over time.

STAY ON TRACK

Assignment and weekly planners help students keep themselves on track (see following page). By working backward, you can establish a timetable for completing the assignment. The planners will become even more effective as you become more familiar with how long it takes to complete the various parts of assignments.

Some students find it helpful to include rewards, such as pub night or pizza and a movie with friends, in their list of activities.

DEAL EFFECTIVELY WITH DISTRACTIONS

The French existentialist philosopher Jean-Paul Sartre (1905-80) once wrote that "Hell is other people." When you're trying to work, and your friends, parents, siblings, or other students want to talk to you or get you to do something with them, you might be tempted to agree. You can keep these interruptions to a minimum by turning off your smartphone and studying in the library. But you'll never eliminate them entirely.

Most people don't understand, don't remember, or conveniently forget the intrusiveness of interruptions and can be offended if you tell them, "Sorry, but I'm working on a project. I'll call you later." How you deal with these disruptions can shape your student experience and even your career. The students and employees who deal firmly but gently with such distractions usually achieve the greatest success, earn the most respect, and go on to become leaders.

On the whole, people tend to have similar levels of intelligence. Individuals who are classified as high achievers or as brilliant are usually not very different from the rest of us. They have learned to focus on the problem at hand and to give it their full attention. To do that, they minimize interruptions.

Here are tips on reducing distractions while keeping your friends:

- Let people know when you are busy and when you will be available.
- Be firm, so that they'll understand that your school work is important to you.

ASSIGNMENT PLANNER

This assignment is due on _____

Component	Time scheduled (hours)	Target date	Done
Background research	4.5		
Developing a thesis/question	1		
Rough outline	3		
Composition	7		
Documentation	2		
Proofreading	3		
Completed assignment	20.5		

WEEKLY PLANNER

Week of _____

Activity	Goal	Component	Time scheduled (hours)	Done
Statistics exam	B	Review readings	3	
		Review notes	1	
		Graphs and tables	1.5	
		Study group meeting	2	
Sociology	B+	Read Chapters 6 and 7	2.5	
		Answer chapter questions	1	
Psychology	A	Attend lab	1.5	
		Read Chapter 5	1.5	
		Q and A session	1	
History	B	Library research	3.5	

▸ Be consistent, so that they'll know where they stand and will realize that you're not rejecting them.

▸ Follow up with them when you're free to do so.

▸ Give them your full attention when you connect with them. That way, they will come to value the *quality* rather than the *quantity* of time that they spend with you.

Make new friends among people whose goals and objectives resemble yours, and who appreciate the importance of focused attention. You can even combine social interaction with academic achievement by forming a study group. Some terrific friendships and future networks get their start in study groups.

One reason for attending university is to meet people and make new friends. The friendships you make at school can, and often do, last a lifetime. It's only when you let your social life interfere too much with your academic life that a problem emerges. Students who learn how to balance their social and academic lives usually do well at university and thereafter.

On the other hand, over-privileging their social life is the main reason why students drop out of university. The temptation can seem overwhelming, especially when students are released from the constraints of high school and parents. That's why it is especially important for those who move away from home and parental controls to develop the internal fortitude that goes with performing well at university.

If you don't possess this ability by the time you hit the workforce, you'll be in trouble. If you are organized, and have the capacity to focus, you already have a good head start on many of your peers.

CHAPTER 3
Prospering in the Classroom and Workplace

Experience is that marvelous thing that enables you to recognize a mistake when you make it again.

— Franklin P. Jones

In this chapter, we will show you how to perform well on exams, essays, and reports while also preparing for similar challenges in your career. Most students, quite logically, spend substantial time preparing for exams and writing essays and other assignments, such as lab reports. Why not use that experience as a springboard to workplace success?

Writing exams, essays, and reports is excellent practice because you'll be faced with important tests in your career and will spend considerable time researching and writing. In fact, the exams in the real world will be of far greater consequence than those in university. If you fail a test in school, your grade may drop, or in the worst-case scenario you may fail a course. Blowing an exam in the labour force may cost you a job, or at least opportunities for advancement (and the associated increase in earnings).

Let's begin with exams.

Exams, a fact of life

You may think that exam writing is the least transferable of university skills. In other words, your exam-writing days are thankfully behind you once you graduate. However, most professionals write many more exams after completing their undergraduate education.

It is not uncommon for job applications to involve written tests. In fact, for many jobs in both the public and private sector – and not just the obvious ones such as police and firefighting – candidates must pass various exams before they're even considered for an interview.

Even if the application for a professional job has no written component, the interview itself is a test – a kind of exam on what you've learned and how well you can organize and present your thoughts and ideas. Doing well in an interview will be difficult if you can't recall important information, respond to unexpected questions, and be analytical.

Many professionals, such as lawyers, accountants, engineers, physiotherapists, and financial advisors, must write qualifying and competency exams. You yourself will probably take courses, paid for by either you or your employer, to earn specific credentials or to learn about new developments in your field. These courses usually involve considerable and lengthy tests.

After you complete your bachelor's degree, you might decide to continue your studies, perhaps by attending law school or taking an MBA or other master's degree. Many of these programs require candidates to pass an entrance exam, such as the LSAT (for law school), GMAT (for business school), or GRE (for graduate school). See Chapter 11 for more on graduate studies.

Finally, you'll face many real-life tests each and every day at work. For instance, your boss may ask you to describe, right now, the underlying problems of your latest project or account. Or a client may call and ask you to explain why his stock has not performed as you suggested it would two years ago. He's in no mood for bullshit, and if you cannot respond to his question, he'll take his business elsewhere. Or Sabrina's father may show up unannounced in your classroom to discuss her progress. If you pass such tests, your colleagues and your boss will regard you positively. If you scramble and flounder, your career will suffer.

REDUCING ANXIETY

Let's face it – exams are anxiety producers. If they don't give you the jitters, pinch yourself, because you're probably dead. Most of the fretting over exams is entirely out of proportion to the significance of the exams themselves, but so what? We are what we feel. Fortunately, we are also what we know. If we can control our nerves and use the exam itself to display our knowledge, we've got a fighting chance of surviving in one piece.

The mere word "exam" strikes terror in the hearts of many students. Years after completing their degrees, graduates sometimes have nightmares about not being able to find the room where an exam is being held. A university instructor merely needs to whisper "This might be on the test" to get the full and undivided attention of a lecture hall of hundreds of students. Even experienced PhD candidates have been reduced to tears while preparing for their exams. Since they've spent so many years in school, you'd think they'd be a bit more comfortable with this exam thing. No way.

You're never going to eliminate exam or performance-related anxiety, either at school or at work, but you can reduce it. It makes sense to begin this process while you're still in school and to carry that lower anxiety into the workforce.

In order of importance, here are the most effective ways of decreasing exam anxiety at university:

▸ *Know your stuff.* Understand the material on which you are being tested. In particular, understand the key ideas or themes in a course and how the facts fit into them.

▸ *Appreciate the positive aspects of stress.* Without stress, we'd have little incentive to perform. Being able to function well under stress is often what separates senior executives from ordinary employees – and strong students from mediocre ones.

▸ *Control excessive stress.* Don't let it paralyze you. Divide your exam preparation into steps. When it all seems overwhelming, get some exercise, watch a movie, or go out for an evening. Learn when to avoid distractions and when to distract yourself productively. Some progressive companies have pool and ping-pong tables in *time-out* rooms, where employees can relax and recharge their batteries.

▸ *Don't cram at the last minute.* We know, we know – it worked in high school, right? Well, it won't work at university and certainly not in your career.

▶ *If you simply must cram, do it intelligently.* Just pack your short-term memory with basic facts, names, and dates, but don't try to learn the key concepts or ideas at the last minute.

▶ *Be aware and stay focused.* Here's where the approach of the Zen master and the good student coincide. You can't be stressed out while you are aware and focused. Enjoy the exam experience. Before you tell us to get real, let us ask a question. When are you most stressed – when you're preparing for an exam or when you sit down and start to write it? Chances are that the stress disappears once you begin to concentrate on the task at hand. Be aware. Appreciate the fact that you've now got something better and more urgent to do than worry.

▶ *Put things in perspective.* An exam is not a life-or-death situation. Believe it or not, many, many people have failed exams and gone on to brilliant careers. One of this book's authors failed his first year of university altogether (here's a hint; his initials are J.A.D.), and the other failed his first-year history course!

PREPARING FOR A BIG EXAM

Not all exams are big exams. Worrying about small tests or spending hours preparing for an exam in an easy course that you're acing is a waste of time. For the big scary exams or career making/breaking moments, however, it's good to have a personal strategy.

Here's a strategy that works for some people and that can be customized to suit your own circumstances:

▶ *Reduce the pressure on yourself.* Concentrate on doing as well as you can rather than aiming for a specific grade. If you are a perfectionist, put your need to be perfect on the back burner for now.

▶ *Forget about the future.* In particular, forget about the impact that the exam might have on your future. Concentrate on the here and now. If you must contemplate the future, think about how relieved you'll be when the exam is over.

▶ *Focus.* Live and breathe exam preparation rather than the exam itself. Exam preparation is not scary; it's just boring.

▶ *Complain like crazy.* Tell all your friends that you are preparing for a big exam and that you won't have a social life (or any life to speak of) until it's over. They'll take the hint and leave you alone, which will allow you to get on with the job. Heck, while you're whining like this, they won't want to be anywhere near you.

▶ *Organize all your study materials and surroundings.* This can be a formal ritual to help you start working. Don't let the organizing take over from the studying, however. Some junior executives stay junior executives because they spend more time tidying up their office than completing the all-important project by deadline.

▶ *Take breaks whether you need them or not.* Studying is an open-ended activity. It stops only when the exam itself begins. This means that you need to schedule regular breaks while studying.

▶ *Identify major gaps in your knowledge early in the preparation process.* Don't wait until the last minute to discover that you don't understand important elements. By then, it will be too late.

▶ *Rewrite your notes.* Reading over your notes is not the most efficient way to prepare for a test. If you *rewrite* them, however, more of the ideas and information will stick, and you will make connections that you might not have spotted before.

Mental clarity and relaxation are often overlooked components for sailing through exams, as well as for engaging in projects that involve critical and creative thinking. Here are keys to relaxing:

▶ *Don't memorize: make understanding your goal.* Memorization is one of the worst ways to organize data. Good exams don't assess your capacity to memorize: they determine how well you understand the material. You may discover that your anxiety level drops once you no longer have to memorize so much.

▶ *Stay loose.* If you have too rigid a script for the challenges of the workplace, you will be inflexible and will find yourself bedeviled by the details. What you want to take to these situations is a good understanding and an open mind so that you can respond to anything you encounter.

▶ *Get a good night's sleep.* On the evening before the exam, tell yourself that you've done all you can. At this point, sleeping well is the best thing you can do for yourself, so you can focus all your energy on the exam itself.

THE BIG DAY

Here are tips to help you do well on exam day:

- Make sure you've got what you need, including extra pens and pencils.
- Get to the examination room early.
- See how nervous everyone is? Misery loves company. You're not the only sufferer.
- Feel good because the pain will soon be over.
- When you open up the exam, relax and take the time to read it all. Don't start writing immediately.
- Pay attention to the marking scheme. You want to identify which questions are worth the most marks and ensure that you don't spend too long on any one area.
- Be strategic. For example, set your sights on finishing the entire exam, rather than getting perfect marks for part of it.
- Focus on the questions. Read them carefully. Read them at least twice. Then read them again.

When translated to the workplace or the boardroom, the advantages of focusing on the task at hand, being prepared, concentrating on what's doable, and being strategic should be obvious.

Strategies for multiple-choice exams

There are few multiple-choice exams in the workplace, which to our minds suggests that they're not the best way of testing understanding or tapping into a person's potential. It is equally doubtful whether much of the real world conforms to the black-and-white model of multiple-choice scenarios. Unfortunately, there are a lot of multiple-choice exams in professional education and in many university subjects. So, whatever the educational validity of multiple-choice tests, you'd better be prepared for them.

Some undergraduate students actually prefer multiple-choice questions to essay questions. However, the drawback of a multiple-choice exam, from the students' point of view, is that the instructor has complete control over the way in which students must demonstrate their knowledge. Usually, there's only one right answer and no shades of grey. Moreover, trick questions abound, because they allow the instructor to see whether students have read questions carefully and have fielded their subtle distinctions.

Studying for a multiple-choice exam is more difficult than studying for any other kind. Multiple-choice exams

▸ require a precise understanding of the material, not simply a reasonable solution to the problem
▸ mix and match course concepts in a confusing manner
▸ reword concepts in ways that force you to think about fine distinctions
▸ play with technicalities, analogies, and comparisons that take time to decipher (but you usually don't have enough time)
▸ oblige you to think about both the structure and the significance of the question.

Because you'll be dealing with so many possible variables during the short exam period, it's essential to have a very clear strategy for this kind of test. In particular, it's important to understand why people do badly on these exams: they read the questions too quickly, get stuck on one or two early on, and pace themselves poorly. Here's advice to help you eliminate or greatly reduce these problems:

▸ *Do all the easy questions first.* Get your brownie points before you tackle anything else. This will make you feel good and will build your confidence, since you'll get most of them right. Spending too much time on the hard questions may prevent you from bagging all the easy ones.

▸ *Read the difficult questions carefully.* Circle the key words. Try to come up with the answer *before* looking at the choices and perhaps becoming confused.

▸ *Then check the choices.* They often trigger an answer. For example, if you know that three answers are incorrect, the remaining one must be right. Some exams include questions whose answers were never mentioned in class. The instructor is expecting you to eliminate choices that you know must be false. Pretty sneaky, eh?

▸ *If you don't know the answer, move on.* The natural tendency is to keep plugging away at a problem, but as they say in the fishing industry, it's sometimes better to cut bait than to stay stuck.

▸ *Look for patterns and similarities.* Obviously, you'll do this for each question as you try to pick the right answer. But do it between the questions as well. It's a rare multiple-choice exam where the answer to one question doesn't hint at the answer to another.

▸ *Take your best guess.* These are not random stabs in the dark. They imply a choice between decreasing levels of probability. Always make certain, however, that marks won't be deducted for errors. In such cases, leave the question blank and move on.

▸ *Do not change answers that are guesses.* This is a waste of time.

▸ *Watch for the most typical traps.* These include qualifiers such as "always" or "never," which usually signal that a choice is too narrowly defined to be the correct answer. Check the questions for double negatives that make the right answer a positive. For example, a double negative such as "not unnecessary" translates to "necessary," and "not impossible" means "possible."

▸ *Review and review again, if you have time.* If you finish early, keep going over the questions. You are guaranteed to find at least one that you screwed up because you read it incorrectly. Also, answers will pop into your head as you discover the links between questions.

Although the educational validity of multiple-choice exams is dubious to say the least, they're often used in professional education because they allow teachers to rank students on a bell curve. If you want to enter a profession or upgrade your professional skills, you will probably run into these sorts of exams periodically. We think that's a shame, but there it is.

Strategies for written exams

Written exams can consist of short-answer questions and essay questions. Short answers are usually easier to write than essays because they tend to test factual recall and can usually be given in point form. Essays are more difficult because they assess your ability, not only to analyze course materials, but also to synthesize them in meaningful ways.

However, essay exams are better at preparing you for your professional career. At work you'll commonly be asked – often at very short notice – to analyze or explain an event, or solve a problem. Why have sales not increased? Why was the crime committed? What will happen to our market share? What should be our global strategy? Why did Sabrina fail her history test?

The advantage of an essay exam is that it puts the ball firmly in your court. You decide how best to answer the question to show off your understanding of the course materials. As the great soccer player Stanley Matthews used to say, he always preferred having the ball because then he knew exactly what he was going to do with it.

Many of the strategies for a written exam are the same as for a multiple-choice exam. You need to read the questions carefully, divide your time appropriately in terms of their worth, and pace yourself.

In addition, you should spend at least 20 percent of your time creating an outline for each essay. This time is well spent, since it allows you to compose your essay quickly and to ensure that it is clearly organized.

There's yet another reason for writing an outline and including it with your examination answers. If you don't manage to finish an essay, the outline will show your marker that you'd mastered the course material, understood the question and knew how to answer it, and were prevented from doing so only because you ran out of time. Many markers will grade a good outline almost as generously as they would a full essay.

To do well on essay exams, you need

▷ a good understanding of the theories and key ideas of the course, and the relationships between the two
▷ strong writing skills, which are discussed later in this chapter
▷ to understand and respond to the question!

Why the exclamation mark? Consider this awful truth – students often fail essay exams because they don't pay attention to the precise language and intent of the question.

This message should be imprinted on your brain: If you don't answer the question, it doesn't matter how much you know, or how much you write, or how much you understand about the general area to which the topic relates. Unless you have a very kind instructor, you will get a big fat zero. Nothing. Nada.

The ability to get to the heart of the question is equally important for professionals. When your boss asks you to tell her about last week's meeting that you attended on her behalf, what does she want (and need) to know? Is it who attended? Or who raised what issues? Or who disagreed with whom? Or why the participants chose a certain strategy? Hey, you have just five minutes, or a page, to respond to her request to "tell me what happened." If you don't give her the appropriate answer, she'll screw up with her boss, and that is bad news for you.

Or, what is a client really asking about his investments? Does he want a detailed explanation of why money was lost? Or is he seeking reassurance that profits will be made in the future? Or is he ensuring that you remember what you told him two years ago? Give him the wrong answer, either in person or by e-mail, because you didn't understand his question, and you'll have one account less.

And what about Sabrina's father? Does he want a detailed question-by-question analysis of her history test? Or is he trying to determine whether you're a good teacher? Or is he after something else entirely? To respond you must begin by understanding his question. Get it wrong, and your principal will start to wonder about you.

If you misread a multiple-choice question, you'll lose only a few marks. But if you misread an essay question on a three-question exam, the best mark that you can possibly achieve is 66 percent. That's why it's so important to read essay exam questions carefully. The rule of thumb is to spend at least ten minutes breaking down the question and ensuring that you've understood it before beginning to write.

To make it even worse, very few essay questions ask you to do simple cut-and-dried things. You won't normally be told to list, describe, identify, or summarize material. And even if you should be so lucky, chances are that the person who wrote the question still expects you to demonstrate such skills as comparing and contrasting, evaluating, organizing in terms of significance, critically analyzing, and synthesizing. The mere fact that you are dealing with an essay question suggests that these activities are included.

Unless you have clear instructions otherwise, be prepared to use your critical skills whenever you confront an essay question. If you're told to trace, outline, illustrate, explain, discuss, criticize or evaluate, interpret, or review, you are being asked to provide a critical analysis (much more on this in the next chapter). The specific meaning of each of these words is less important than the general activity required.

Still, it's useful to think about the distinctions between these words because they give you hints about what your teacher (or employer) wants:

▶ To *trace* is to show the evolution of something from start to finish.
▶ To *outline* is to focus on the main components of something.
▶ To *illustrate* is to provide concrete examples to support an argument.
▶ To *explain* is to give the reasons for or causes of something.
▶ To *discuss* is to weigh the pros and cons of something.
▶ To *criticize* or *evaluate* is to assess the merit of something in considerable depth.
▶ To *interpret* is to find a deeper meaning or underlying pattern in something.
▶ To *review* is to go over an event or explanation so as to analyze it in a fresh way.

But the subtle differences between these words pale in comparison to the fact that you'll be expected to provide a critical analysis that breaks down the various parts of an issue to reveal causes, connections, and interrelationships. If you want to excel, you must show not only that you can think, but also that you can think creatively and imaginatively.

In the same way, your co-workers and boss will be looking for ongoing evidence that you are critical, creative, and imaginative in whatever task you undertake. Employers certainly won't pay you a great salary to be unoriginal or to repeat common sense knowledge. No, they want in-depth analysis, concise explanations, and plausible options that add value. Just like your professors!

Essay exams encourage you to play with concepts, build on the theories of others, and create your own interpretations and syntheses. Just as importantly, they force you to demonstrate these complex skills while meeting a deadline. Lots of people can perform decently if they're given enough time, but the competitive employment market is full of deadlines. There's a reason why the word "dead" appears in deadlines: if you can't meet or beat them, your career will soon be six feet under.

Below is a breakdown of three key words that you will most frequently encounter when writing essays for exams and take-home assignments. The three words – compare, argue, and assess – are important because they hint at the kind of critical skills that teachers and employers want.

Compare	Argue	Assess
To compare means to focus on the similarities, differences, and links between ideas. Your comparison should reveal that you fully understand the implications of the ideas.	To bolster your argument, address the alternatives directly. Don't rely on setting up a *straw man* – a point that you create solely for the purpose of knocking it down.	To assess means to sift through arguments and evidence, using scholarly criteria to build a case. It also implies that your case will show how well you understand the issues.

To answer questions that ask you to compare, argue, or assess, follow this guide.[4]

Compare: focus on similarities, but take note of differences.	**Argue:** state precisely the thesis or hypothesis that you intend to prove.	**Assess:** explore the range of positions and debates on an issue.
Contrast: focus on differences, but be aware of similarities.	**Prove:** use logic and evidence to establish the validity of your thesis.	**Evaluate:** indicate both their strengths and weaknesses.

Connect: show how the ideas are related to each other.

Debate: test your argument against other possible alternatives.

Interpret: simplify complexities so that these issues can be communicated.

Evaluate: if you compare ideas, it is implied that you will evaluate them.

Justify: show why your argument is better.

Judge: assess the merit, accuracy, or usefulness of differing approaches.

Do you see how someone who can compare, argue, and assess under the pressure of a tight deadline would be valuable to an organization? If that individual could also make accurate judgments, wouldn't he or she be indispensable? Now add to that the ability to convince others by constructing a logical argument and using relevant data to support each claim, and you've got yourself a worker to die for!

The usefulness of essays

Being able to answer "why" questions is essential at both school and work. In university and your chosen profession, this form of question far outnumbers all the other kinds. The higher you move in your occupation, the more your bosses, colleagues, clients, customers, and stakeholders will expect you to address the question *why*. Why did my stocks go down? Why are sales up this quarter? Why do we have fewer clients this year? Why does he want to see me? Why is the project not finished? Why is my daughter not doing well in grade two?

Of course, you'll field other questions as well – What stocks should I buy? What should I teach my students? – but these too will involve explaining why your answer is the best one.

Thus, the most critical skill to learn in university is how to explain things. In other words, you must learn how to provide others with a convincing *interpretation* that explains a particular development or event. And not just any old development or event, but complex subjects that are difficult to understand.

At some point during your university career, you will write at least one essay. You probably won't be asked to do this at work, so, quite legitimately, you may feel that the effort required for essays is somewhat wasted, or at least not particularly transferable. However, many employers expect job applicants to submit a cover letter, the purpose of which is to answer the question "Why should we hire you for this position?" Interviews often include short written questions. Applications for graduate programs all require statements of interest that reply to "Why should we accept you into this program?"

Essays enable you to sharpen your ability to answer "why" questions and significantly improve your aptitude for communicating your findings. Your boss won't ask you to write an essay regarding why sales have dropped this quarter, but she will want a report that explains why this occurred and that recommends how to reverse the trend. What's more, she'll want you to demonstrate the critical and creative thinking that essay writing builds. The topics of critical and creative thinking are explored in more detail in the next chapter, as well as in Chapters 7 and 8.

Essay writing teaches you to *explain* things to others. It doesn't matter whether the subject is Byzantine architecture or commodity investments. The interpretive, critical, and analytical skills will be the same regardless of the topic of your essay.

Ever wonder how your university professors got so smart and so good at understanding and explaining difficult things? They wrote a hell of a lot of essays, case studies, or reports. Once they finished their undergraduate degree, they didn't stop writing essays. To become professors, they usually had to write a PhD thesis. A thesis is just a really long, original, and informed essay. Once they get to be professors, they have to write articles (shorter essays) and books (longer essays) to keep their jobs and be promoted. You didn't think that they spent all their time teaching, did you?

You probably don't plan on becoming a professor – at least not just yet – but you can develop the same critical and creative skills for use in your chosen career. Use your essays to practise generating concise, well-grounded, and interesting explanations and arguments. Sometimes settling on an essay topic can be difficult, especially if your professor or teaching assistant lets you choose your own. You can solve this problem by selecting a topic that works to your advantage after graduation. Essays and similar assignments give you the opportunity to explore the kind of career you want. Use them to become an expert in a particular field.

For instance, why not study how a new free trade agreement affects Canada, specifically Canadian companies or workers? Or, if a certain issue is prominent in the media (such as a discovery, a debate, or a tragedy), why not study an aspect of it for your humanities, social science, or other courses? When you start your job search, even for summer or part-time positions, you can show potential employers that you have specialized and current knowledge of these current developments and changes.

You can also study an emerging trend. For instance, the Canadian population is aging as the baby-boom generation begins to turn sixty-five. This trend will affect many aspects of Canadian life, from product development to health care policy and pensions. If during your university career, you write several papers on the aging population, you will have knowledge that employers will value. The brilliant thing is that most organizations will have to deal with the aging population, whether they are auto manufacturers, banks, or travel agencies.

Now might be a good occasion for Nike and Adidas to move some of their assets out of jogging equipment and into golf clubs and apparel. Not many older people will persist with long-distance running, because it's hard on aging joints! Book publishers will have a bonanza once more retired people have time to read. But will they read printed books, e-books, or something else? What kind of material is of interest to older consumers?

Selecting essay and research topics that are relevant to you and potential employers can be done in any discipline, including philosophy, history, and English. Scandals in government, fraud in business, crime rates, and the rights of individuals raise some of the key questions that philosophers study.

Another beneficial outcome is that you can take your completed research paper to your interview. See Chapter 9 for more on the interview process.

As we noted earlier in this book, it's crucial to take courses that appeal to you. But why not move that interest a step further and pick essay topics that engage you? Then be strategic and look for links between your interests and the kind of subjects that might appeal to future employers or provide a foundation for a future career. Writing essays, especially good ones, is work, but it's enjoyable if it relates to your interests.

You can build your own unique interests into a smart career strategy. Once you have identified a particular area of interest, explore it through a variety of courses. Over time, you will know more about the subject than most other people. This makes you something of an expert, and ultimately more marketable.

It's not enough to be interested in a subject. You need to approach it in a rigorous way. Academic writing, and especially scientific writing, is the most objective kind of prose. The academic writer has a particular obligation to communicate information that is as precise, unbiased, and correct as possible. Hyperbole and overly dramatic wording are not part of good academic writing, because they detract from the simple efficiency of the language and prevent clear communication.

Clear communication is absolutely essential in the workplace. Professional and business writing must be objective if it is to be effective. A report that is dramatic or contains inflated language, or is biased or inaccurate, will result in poor decisions. Decisions are (or should be) grounded solely in facts, evidence, logic, and level-headedness. You must be able to write in this manner to succeed in a profession. There is no better way of learning how to do it than by crafting a university essay, report, or case study.

Health care and legal specialists, accountants, social workers, police officers, nurses, teachers, journalists, and many other professionals must be objective and impartial. When they write or speak, they do so only after carefully weighing and analyzing the facts, and considering a possible hypothesis to explain them. That doesn't mean that they can't have an opinion. It does mean that they need to clearly *articulate* that opinion, *support* it with theories and evidence, and *defend* it against other plausible opinions.

Students sometimes complain that professors are "too picky" or "should have known" what was meant in an essay. Adopting this attitude about grades has no place in an academic environment, because academic writing is all about precision and clarity. Stylistic and grammatical errors, and faulty logic, are penalized because bad writing obscures meaning and impedes effective communication.

Unsupported arguments are questioned, not because your professor necessarily disagrees with you, but because such writing is unscholarly. In the professional world, you'll be expected to back up every statement you make. If you have a tendency to make statements without thinking or on the basis of emotion/intuition, your employers and colleagues will label you a loose cannon. The problem with loose cannons is that they're inaccurate and can even threaten the harmony of the ship. As a result, they tend to be dismissed or demoted to jobs where they can't do much damage.

A professor may give you some leeway if you muddle your argument, or provide insufficient evidence, or write weakly. After all, university is a place to learn, and that means making mistakes. However, you can bet that the person who pays your salary and possibly relies on your expertise in very tangible ways won't cut you any slack at all.

Writing for the academic reader

Whenever you write, whatever you write, keep your audience in mind. Many students fall into the trap of trying to write for a particular instructor and waste time figuring out what will please him or her. Some students even go so far as *pretending* to support the ideas or theories that their teacher holds.

This is usually a misguided approach. It may work with one or two instructors, but it's a low-percentage strategy. It's far wiser to apply your energy to constructing an academically sound argument. At least this way you'll gain the skills that will make you a better writer at the university level.

Every year, the authors of this book have to give low marks to students who simply parrot what they think we want to hear rather than carefully researching and developing a position. It's difficult to respect people who engage in this form of flattery and don't want to learn for themselves.

The same thing goes for the workplace. Most bosses don't like yes-men or yes-women. Sure, you can write reports and memos that are designed to please your boss, but that won't work for long. Once you get a reputation for being a bootlicker, your boss won't respect you and your colleagues won't trust you. Your career will be seriously damaged, and you may even have difficulty hanging on to your self-respect. It's much better to learn to write in a professional manner that suits the environment in which you work.

Every academic essay is expected to include the following seven qualities:

1 *Completeness and comprehensiveness.* Academic writers must clearly locate their work within a body of knowledge, demonstrate how it contributes to that knowledge, and proceed from a statement of the problem to its resolution.

A common saying in the workplace is "Don't reinvent the wheel." When you write, build on the knowledge that already exists.

2 *Accuracy.* Academic writers must provide accurate information. This means that they must check all their statements to ensure that they are not obscuring the data or jumping to false conclusions. Accuracy in essay writing demands that students choose their words carefully and expect to be challenged on any claims that cannot be verified.

If you fudge the data, your employers and superiors will be particularly harsh with you because it could result in incorrect decisions and embarrassing situations, or much worse.

3 *Impartiality.* Academic writing is impartial. Academic writers – whether students or professors – usually state their theoretical frameworks or biases right away, so that readers can assess the presentation of the data for themselves. They inform readers of the limitations of their work and tell them about other interpretations that they have rejected. They don't exaggerate the importance of their findings. Most of all, they never sweep inconvenient data under the carpet.

Similarly, your employer or superior, colleagues, co-workers, and clients rely on impartial information. As they decide how to proceed, they usually take many factors into account, including other options. However, if their decision is based on biased information, the outcome will be doomed from the start.

4 *Order.* Beginning writers often have trouble organizing their thoughts on paper. Academic writing presents material in a logical order. Difficult or problematic data are introduced carefully, and unnecessary information is omitted so that the flow of the discussion isn't disrupted. Every section of the essay needs to be structured clearly, and the transition between sections must demonstrate coherent development. The ideas and information in each paragraph should be related to each other.

Academic writing typically follows chronological order to avoid hurling the reader back and forth in time, such as from present, to past, to present, to future, and to past. As we note a little later in this chapter, editing is crucial to attain a logical and orderly final product.

Order and logical development are crucial in the world of business and government. Usually, documents are headed by an abstract, or executive summary, that condenses the argument but also shows how the points tie together. If any links are loose or missing, the entire report is rejected. You may not be asked to write abstracts at university, but you can include them with your papers nonetheless. Not only will this let you practise the important skill of summarizing a long document in a few hundred words, it will also impress your professor or teaching assistant and, perhaps, increase your grade.

5 *Relevance.* Why do students have problems with the order of their material? Some don't organize their research findings clearly. Some are so eager to show off how hard they worked and how much they know that they jam everything into an essay, even if it's not relevant to the assignment.

In the past, you may have been rewarded for tenacity and the ability to remember information. At the university level, we *expect* you to do the work, but we *reward* you for clarity and relevance. That's why you may get a much lower mark than someone who has done far less work and may even know less about the subject.

Employers simply do not tolerate irrelevant or off-track thinking. They pay employees to focus on the problem at hand, and any digression wastes both their money and their time.

Here's a business axiom that may help you: don't just work, work smart.

6 *Simplicity.* Academic writing should demonstrate that you have mastered the material and can communicate it effectively. University teachers will challenge you if your words and ideas are not simple and straightforward. The best way to show that you understand subtle and complex ideas is to put them into simple language.

The authors of this book have written many documents for large public- and private-sector organizations, both national and international. We aimed to write with the utmost simplicity and often had to revise the text many times before it reached that goal.

7 *Clarity.* Following the six steps above will produce clarity, which is all about making the complex simple. Clarity is about distinguishing between logical arguments and emotional appeals. Clarity is getting rid of irrelevancies so that you can communicate with greater precision. Clarity lives in focused and elegant language, rather than flowery, long-winded, or convoluted prose. Lastly, clarity is explaining something effectively right off the bat, rather than repeating it unnecessarily.[5]

If you reread the seven points above, you will see that each one applies to any writing you will do outside of university. Who would take you seriously if your sales presentation, memorandum, legal brief, or child custody case report were not accurate, or comprehensive, or relevant, or impartial, or concise? Will your professional colleagues, managers, clients, and others value your ideas, comments, and suggestions if they don't meet the guidelines above?

In an environment where time is money, and where your superiors need to make sound decisions based on good information, you will need the skills that come from good essay writing. It is no coincidence that the best writers at university also attain the most promising post-graduation careers.

How to organize an essay

Organizing your essay is different from organizing your research, which is structured in terms of topics and sub-topics. Of course, these will form the critical substance and argument of your essay. The meat of your essay is contained in your research (see

Chapter 6 for more). But good academic essays also follow certain organizational conventions that readers have come to expect.

When you pick up a novel, you expect it to use a certain kind of structure. Poems take various forms as well, depending on whether they are sonnets, elegies, or epics. Plays usually have a certain number of acts that vary according to when they were written and the cultural norms in which they were produced. Similarly, academic essays usually feature one or more of the following structures.

ARGUMENTATIVE

Many scholarly essays and articles take the form of arguments or debates. An argumentative essay must develop a clear thesis – an argument – that is supported with evidence. It typically begins by outlining its thesis. Then it describes one or more conflicting arguments. After evaluating their merits, it shows why its thesis is best.

The reader (your professor) will be looking for evidence that you fully understand both the strengths and the weaknesses of the approaches with which you disagree.

INTERPRETIVE

An interpretive essay uses sophisticated tools to illuminate the topic at hand. These may be disciplinary approaches, such as modernism or postmodernism, or they may be theoretical models, such as Freudianism or Marxism. In applying them, the essay interprets or makes sense of material. This type of essay can go well beyond common sense or intuition in discovering the patterns and deep meanings in material, and is thus one of the most valuable tools available to scholars.

Your reader will want to see that you understand the theoretical frameworks and can apply them properly. Many students try to use theories without understanding them – with predictable results.

DESCRIPTIVE

A descriptive essay is one that avoids interpreting material or pursuing an argument. Its purpose is merely to outline a process or convey factual information that will be useful to the reader. It requires the careful selection of relevant facts as well as clear and concise communication.

The reader will be asking, "What's missing from this picture?" You can't include everything in a descriptive essay, but be sure not to overlook anything important.

COMPARATIVE/EXPLORATORY

A comparative essay is one that takes two different approaches to a problem or question. These can be theoretical frameworks such as Freudianism and Marxism, or they can be two viewpoints regarding a controversial issue such as abortion or affirmative action. Both approaches are discussed and one is usually preferred to the other.

The reader wants to see that you have understood the comparative strengths and weaknesses of the two approaches, and that you have a good reason for rejecting one of them. Avoid trying to score points by setting up a straw man, a weak argument that's designed solely to be torn down. A perceptive reader will recognize that it doesn't really engage with the material.

INCREMENTAL

An incremental essay is one that slowly builds from small, seemingly insignificant points to a powerful conclusion. Each step builds on the previous one to create an impressive edifice.

The reader will be looking for missing steps.

SYNTHETIC

A synthetic essay uses the most appropriate and relevant elements of the various essay types discussed above to create the strongest argument possible. Good academic arguments are complex and subtle, and they rarely rely on just one approach.

The reader, who appreciates the difficulty of making synthetic arguments, will check whether you've done a good job of applying the relevant theories and approaches to gain insights into the material.

If you reread our discussion of essay types, you will see that each one has its counterpart in professional settings. At some time during your career, you will probably be asked to write a report that analyzes two different business strategies and argues in favour of one. Or you may have to explain why a particular project failed. Or you may simply be expected to describe the facts as they are.

Good reports or business case studies often contain elements from all the essay types. They may begin with a clear and detailed description of a situation or problem. They may build information incrementally and logically to establish a pattern. At some point, they will apply theories and interpretations to generate options or alternatives. They may bring theories and approaches together in unique ways to provide a creative solution, recommendation, or interpretation.

The basic structure of an essay

The basic structure of an essay or a professional report is simplicity itself. It consists of a beginning, a middle, and an end. The beginning introduces your subject. The middle develops the various steps in your argument and proves the claims that you made in the introduction. The conclusion sums up what you have argued, proved, and discovered. It may also include any future implications of your findings.

YOUR ESSAY'S INTRODUCTION

Getting started is half the battle. Don't make it any harder than it already is. You don't need a dynamic opening to get going. You just need to introduce your topic – the problem, question, or dilemma – followed by any necessary background, and tell the reader what you intend to prove or show. In other words, this section identifies the major problem, controversy, debate, or question to be examined in the essay.

Although this section is brief, it needs to show the value of what is to follow. Depending on the complexity of your topic, the introduction can take up just one paragraph or a couple of pages. There are no absolute rules regarding its length.

Many of you will have had the concept of a thesis statement drilled into your heads. A lot of writing guides insist that the thesis statement must spell out exactly what the essay intends to prove.

Although this advice is well meant, it's nonsense. Some of the greatest essays and most influential reports ever written don't follow this rule.

Many professors expect a paper to include a traditional thesis statement. If this applies to you, be sure to provide one. If not, what you really want to do is create a controlling statement that comes early in your introduction or that you clearly and concisely build toward. It doesn't have to be a thesis statement. It can present the question that you intend to answer, the problem that you'll be solving, or the dilemma that you'll explore.

Students commonly provide the answer to the question, problem, or dilemma in their introduction. Can you imagine a mystery novel whose very first sentence revealed that "the butler did it"? The controlling statement of a mystery novel, which is so well known that it's often implied rather than actually expressed, is "Who did it?" The controlling sentence also provides the framework and main organizing principle for the entire book.

In your introduction, it's okay to keep the reader in a bit of suspense. You need to explain your essay topic, but you don't need to spill all the beans at once. Say, for example, that your paper is on the impact of the aging population on the design of cars. In the introduction, you probably don't want to state what the impact will be: instead, raise the subject as a potentially important and interesting one. Try to hook the reader. Once hooked, he or she will want to learn how the aging population will affect auto design, as argued by you and supported by the evidence that you uncovered during your research.

A common mistake of novice students is to create a thesis statement before they've even done any research and then to force all the evidence to support it. The mythical Greek bandit known as Procrustes, who forced travellers to lie in an iron bed, did something similar. If his victims were too short to fit, he stretched them. If they were too tall, he cut off their legs. Don't make yourself a Procrustean bed!

The introduction ends with a short paragraph that outlines the rest of the essay. Say something like, "The first section of this paper will ... The second section will ..." Providing an outline at this point means that reading your essay won't feel like being on a roller-coaster ride while wearing a blindfold. Briefly tell the reader what to expect. Using subheadings in the main part of the paper can sometimes be helpful.

YOUR ESSAY'S BODY

You can literally count the number of paragraphs that you need in your essay by adding up two things – your major arguments and the concepts that you need to develop. The usual rule of thumb is that you need at least one paragraph for each concept. These key building blocks are essential in structuring an essay. If you were writing an economics paper, for example, you might discuss the concepts of self-interest, competition, private property, and profits. We'll have a lot more to say about concepts in the next chapter. In the meantime, we'll confine ourselves to their organization.

If you've done your research well, all of the concepts should already be organized in a computer file, in your mind, or on index cards. It's not a bad idea to put the concepts on sticky notes or cards so that you can move them around as you begin to compose your essay. No matter how thoroughly you've organized your research, the process of writing will result in a further reshuffling of your thoughts. Sticky notes allow you to play with concepts without being stuck (if you'll pardon the pun) in one permanent location.

The structure and size of each paragraph depend on how much you need to write to develop each concept. As long as you cover the territory adequately, it doesn't matter whether the paragraphs are long or short. In certain instances, you'll find that you have less to say about some of the concepts. To flesh them out, you may need to do a bit more research.

Concepts are linked together to form arguments. Your primary guide in deciding whether your information and concepts are developed enough is the logical sequence of your argument. As you compose the body of your essay, constantly reread the paragraphs to ensure that they flow in a logical progression.

You can determine whether your essay flows by asking the following questions:

▸ Can I move backward and forward logically from any point in my discussion?

▸ Can I quickly diagram my essay on a blackboard or a piece of paper?

▸ Can I add greater subtlety or complexity without disrupting the flow?

YOUR ESSAY'S CONCLUSION

Although your teaching assistant or professor will read your entire paper, its conclusion must nonetheless follow logically and clearly from its introduction. You will know that these sections are both strong and complete when you can read just the two of them (omitting the rest) and comprehend the essence of the paper. Moreover, if some concepts and arguments in the body of your essay are obscure or confusing, a strong introduction and conclusion will help carry your reader through them.

Sometimes in the business world, only the introduction and conclusion of a professional document will be read carefully. Busy senior executives often skim or browse the rest. That's why it's good practice to be extraordinarily clear, concise, and precise in your introductions and conclusions.

One of the genuine tragedies in otherwise intelligent and well-composed essays is a poor conclusion. Many students sabotage their efforts by doing one of the following:

▸ failing to write a proper conclusion ("Thank god it's over!")
▸ introducing new ideas or material ("Oh, by the way")
▸ being undecided or wishy-washy ("I'm confused").

The first of these offences is perhaps understandable. By the time you've developed all your points, you'll probably feel that your job is done. Wrong! You need to write a neat recap of what you've proven or uncovered, or at least underline its significance. There's nothing more irritating than an essay that builds toward a climax but never gets there. This is the academic equivalent of people who don't finish their sentences but assume that you'll know what they meant to say.

The second offence – introducing new ideas or information – is inexcusable. You may be tempted to add more, but this is not the place to do it. Although you're permitted to suggest directions for future research, your conclusion should contain nothing else that's new.

Breaking this rule completely takes your reader's mind off the argument that you've just spent several pages trying to prove. Even worse, it raises questions about what else might be missing from the essay.

Usually, students (and writers in general) add new information and ideas at the end because they discovered them just as they finished up their essay. The secret, or not so secret, means to avoid this situation is not to write the paper at the last minute. That way, if new ideas do occur to you, or you find interesting new facts that are too important to ignore, you still have time to integrate them into the essay itself.

Another way to avoid adding new information in the conclusion is to deal with a tightly focused or narrow topic, question, problem, or dilemma in your essay. Using a general, vague, or broad controlling statement will, quite naturally, produce more information than can handily be included in your discussion.

Early in the essay you can easily write that, for example, events in China were crucial to the Vietnam War but that you won't be considering them, perhaps due to lack of space. This is far better than waiting until the last paragraph and suddenly revealing that developments in China were critical to the Vietnam War. A good rule of thumb is never to use "also" or "in addition" in the last page or two of an essay.

The third offence – being uncertain or vague in the conclusion – is sometimes hard to avoid. Wanting to play it safe in case the paper might have omitted something crucial, or might not be perfect, or because you don't really trust your arguments or findings, is natural. Nevertheless, an indecisive ending is a letdown for the reader, who has followed your discussion from start to finish.

You will know that your conclusion is effective if you feel a sense of closure when you review it. Both you and your reader should feel *been there, done that*. Don't leave any loose ends!

We can tell you that the business world has zero tolerance for indecision. If you compose a case study for your boss, you dare not sit on the fence. People in business must make hard decisions within strict deadlines; they don't have the luxury of fence sitting. So it's a good idea to start getting your butt off the fence right now!

Essay writing as a process

Essay and report writing takes time. It's a process, not a mysterious event that occurs on the night before a deadline. As explained below, that process consists of producing more than one draft, polishing the final version, citing sources, and choosing an appropriate title.

THE FIRST DRAFT

You'll do most of your hard work in creating the first draft of your essay or report. It's where you integrate thinking, research, and writing to craft an argument that

- establishes a clear thesis, problem, or dilemma
- addresses and solves a legitimate problem
- demonstrates the effective use of evidence
- reflects your own perspective
- establishes one or more memorable points (for yourself and your reader).

Accomplishing all these goals isn't easy, even for experienced writers. At some point in the draft stage, you will almost certainly run into a mental roadblock. When this happens, you can help yourself out by

- jumping to a different part of the essay, where the writing might flow more easily
- taking a break, relaxing, and allowing ideas to come without forcing them
- completing mechanical things such as your title and reference pages

- writing down what you know and not worrying about what you don't know
- talking to a teacher or other student about the difficult section
- going back and doing more research.

When you're blocked, learning to relax without putting your essay completely out of your mind is the most useful thing you can do. As long as even a small part of your mind remains connected to the paper, your subconscious will work on the problem and the solution will often just come to you. If you try too hard, your subconscious can't solve the problem for you. Conversely, if you entirely let go of the problem, it may be even bigger when you come back to it.

It's a very good idea to get into the habit of carrying a notebook (paper or electronic), in which you can jot down insights as they occur to you. Experienced professional writers do this as a matter of course. Many even keep a pad and pencil, tablet, or cellphone on the bedside table to record any revelations that pop up in the middle of the night. Nothing is more annoying than going back to sleep and finding that your idea has completely evaporated by the next morning!

THE SECOND DRAFT

A great writer was once asked to explain the secret of her success. Her answer was immediate and simple: rewriting. If you were to apply a cost-benefit analysis to essay writing, it would show that devoting a day to revision has the biggest payoff. Here are tips to guide rewriting:

- Always wait for a couple of days before you write the second draft; if it's too fresh in your mind, you won't be able to spot any problems objectively.
- Examine what you've written as though it were a classmate's essay rather than your own work.
- Check the transitions between paragraphs. Are they smooth and helpful to the reader?
- Read your essay aloud to determine whether it makes sense and flows well.

Reading your work aloud is an extremely effective communication strategy. Here are a few things you can discover about your paper, simply by reading it aloud:

▶ its overall effect, tone, and flow
▶ whether it's focused or unfocused
▶ where the gaps are
▶ which arguments work and which don't
▶ whether it repeats itself.

This strategy can be even more effective if you tape the reading and then listen to the playback.

It's not a good idea to focus on spelling or the rules of grammar during this stage. Once you begin a word-by-word edit, you simply can't engage in creative problem solving at the same time. You also lose the ability to see your essay from the point of view of an interested reader.

THE FINAL DRAFT

The final draft is the right place to do the close editing that every paper needs. Now is the time to go over grammar, punctuation, spelling, and word choice. Computer spell checkers certainly make the final editing process a lot easier than formerly, but they can miss and mislead. It's up to you to perform the close and careful check that can make the difference between a B+ and an A.

Students often wonder why they are penalized for mistakes that have nothing to do with thinking. Here are four reasons:

▶ Spelling errors and typos are signs of sloppiness, rushing, and lack of attention.
▶ A limited vocabulary prevents you from saying what you really mean.
▶ Poor punctuation detracts from the flow of your essay, making the reader go over the sentence more than once.
▶ Weak grammar reduces the force of a sentence or paragraph and often changes or garbles its meaning.

There is little tolerance for grammatical mistakes in anything that you write for an organization or company. Your superiors don't get paid for locating and fixing your spelling errors. An extra zero or faulty work in a document can have legal, financial, and personal repercussions for both you and your employer.

EDITING

It is very difficult, and often impossible, to edit your own prose. It's hard to find the problems, both grammatical and substantive, in your writing. No author can possibly edit his or her own work expertly.

With editing, you need to enlist the help of your colleagues. In a professional environment, these would be your co-workers or a paid copy editor. For an essay, try to assemble two sets of editors: The first one will read the second draft and give advice on problems with logic, structure, arguments, and so forth. The second set will read the final draft and will look only at writing problems.

A common mistake is to ask family and friends to read over your essay. These people will naturally want to be supportive and are likely to respond with "Darling, this is the best thing you've ever written." Such comments are not helpful. Find colleagues who are critical, who will question you, and who will point out flaws, problems, inconsistencies, and any other form of weakness. When you find such people, or when you've trained them, treat them very well. Their input will considerably improve your essay grade.

Incidentally, the best way to keep good editors is to reciprocate. They will give your papers as much attention as you give theirs. If you are not as good a writer or editor as they are, reciprocate in other ways.

Many blue-chip companies have collaborative strategies for editing important letters and documents, all of which will be seen and commented on by several people at each stage of the writing process. Each person is expected to take his or her editorial responsibilities extremely seriously, and the group as a whole comes under scrutiny if someone falls down on the job. No government document or letter is ever released to the public unless at least six people read and edit it.

CITING SOURCES

Many essay writers have problems with citing material from books, articles, and the Internet. The general rule is that you must reference both ideas and facts that you acquired from other people, whether you include them in the form of a quote or rephrase them in your own words. If you are copying material (that is, copying and pasting), you must put it in quotation marks to show that the words are not your own and to reveal your source.

If you are directed to use a particular citation style, either that developed by the American Psychological Association (APA) or the Modern Language Association (MLA), be sure to apply it throughout. If you're at liberty to choose a style, use just one and be consistent. If you're unsure, simply adopt whatever style is used in your textbook or other key books or articles in the course.

Perhaps the easiest way of citing a source is by using the author-date style. The examples below give three different ways of using an author-date citation in a sentence:

> One writer argues that retirement is a central transition in the life of individuals, which also has wider impacts in society (Klassen 2013).
>
> Klassen (2013, 1) states that retirement from work "is a significant event in the life cycle; more broadly, it has impacts on the workplace, the labour market, the economy and society."
>
> One position is that retirement has broad "impacts on the workplace, the labour market, the economy and society," and that it also affects individuals and their families (Klassen 2013, 1).

Your list of references will include the following entry:

> Klassen, Thomas R. (2013). *Retirement in Canada.* Don Mills, ON: Oxford University Press.

If you found this book on the Internet, add the link at the end of the entry, such as http://www.amazon.ca/Retirement-Canada-Thomas-R-Klassen/dp/0199005745. Give the date that you read it, such as "accessed on 14 March 2015."

Citing sources completely and accurately is extremely important in government and business, where an infringement on intellectual property rights could result in lawsuits, other sanctions, and
dismissal from employment. At the very least, an employee who
fails to cite sources completely and accurately will be disciplined,
whether formally or informally.

DON'T FORGET THE TITLE PAGE

When you perform your final edit, don't forget the title of your
paper. Regardless of its length or content, every essay or report
should have a unique, meaningful, and engaging title. The title
should not simply reword the assignment question but should give
the reader some insight into what the paper contains. A thoughtful and intriguing title puts the reader in the right frame of mind
when starting to read.

The title page also includes basic information such as the date,
course number, your name and student number, and the name of
the professor, teaching assistant, or marker. Make it interesting
(perhaps with a graphic or image) since it sets the tone for the rest.
It is always a good idea to ask your teacher whether he or she has
any specific preferences, however, since some do not like diagrams,
graphics, or unusual fonts.

At this stage, you may also want to consider – if you haven't
done so already – whether adding an interesting quotation on the
first page of the essay might be suitable. Many authors find this
a good way of gaining the attention and interest of readers. You
may have noticed that every chapter in this book is headed with a
quote. All of them were chosen carefully for meaning and relevance. Last but not least, also ensure that you have numbered the
pages in your paper.

Common essay-writing errors

If you need extra work in English grammar, seek help from your
university's writing centre or a private tutor. Don't hesitate to do
this, as you'll swiftly improve your writing skills and your grades!
Moreover, grammar is learned quickly, so the necessary investment

in time (and money) will be small, but will remain with you for the rest of your life.

Here are some mistakes in both university and professional writing.

OVERUSE OF THE PASSIVE VOICE

The following sentence contains two examples of the passive voice: "The meeting was called to order, and the budget was presented." Rewritten to use the active voice, the sentence reads, "The president called the meeting to order, and the treasurer presented the budget." Sometimes it's difficult to avoid the passive voice. Using it too much, however, significantly reduces the clarity and force of your thoughts. Students often employ passive constructions to evade identifying the subject of a sentence. For example, a student might write, "This was seen to be an important problem." A good marker will ask, "By whom?"

PRONOUNS

Always check your pronouns (words such as he, it, one, and they) to ensure that they agree with each other. That is, don't begin a passage by referring to, say, "they" and then switch to "he." If you start with a singular noun, stick to it. A sentence such as "The writer submitted their paper" is grammatically incorrect, though this type of error is very common. Also, avoid using pronouns in a vague manner. For instance, saying "It was good last night" leaves the reader in the dark about what might have been good.

TENSE CONFUSION

Perhaps the most common, and most distracting, grammatical error is the incorrect use of tenses. This forces readers to go back over the sentence to ensure that they've understood it. If your essay begins with the past tense, it needs to continue in this tense (unless there's a logical reason to change it). In any case, always be aware of what tense you're using.

CONVOLUTED PHRASING

Convoluted sentences can arise because material is complex or a writer is confused. But they are commonly grounded in an effort to sound academic. They are often accompanied by the use of the passive voice, making them even more unwieldy and confusing. Aim to be as clear as possible, keep your sentences crisp and lean, prune out the deadwood, and remember that although something may sound clear to you, it's the reader who counts.

INAPPROPRIATE AND MISSING WORDS

Poorly chosen or missing words, often the result of too much cutting and pasting, usually indicate that a paper was written in a hurry. They're like a red flag, and what they tell your teacher (or employer) is that you wrote your text at the last minute. They usually convey that old familiar expression – "I don't really give a shit!"

Trust us, you don't want to give that impression, so reread your work to ensure that everything is as perfect as you can make it.

POSSESSIVE USE

Many people have difficulty with the possessive form, but it's easy to master with a little practice. Remember that most possessive nouns take an apostrophe – as in the "robins' nest" or the "cat's pajamas." Note that in these examples, the apostrophe comes after the "s" in the plural noun (robins') and before the "s" in the singular noun (cat's). The possessive form is often muddled with the simple plural, perhaps because many people can't remember the rule but are vaguely aware that words ending in "s" often have an apostrophe. Thus, it's very common to see street signs or magazine ads that refer to, say, "flower's for sale" or "price's slashed."

There are always exceptions that complicate any rule, especially in English. Perhaps the worst confusion arises in the case of "its" versus "it's." "Its" is the possessive form, e.g., "The company failed to meet *its* profit targets" or "The cat chased *its* tail." "It's" is a shortened version of "it is" or "it has," e.g., "*It's* a well-paying summer job at York University. I think *it's* already been posted on the website."

"THIS SOUNDS JUST FINE TO ME"

Students occasionally try to defend an error by saying that it was acceptable in high school. We've got news for you – you're not in high school any more. Though no one likes to be criticized for his or her writing, especially if the experience is new, university and the workplace can be very critical.

We've had some students look at the red ink on their marked papers and complain that they seem to be "bleeding"! Some claim that their professors or teaching assistants are too picky. You can be certain that your managers, clients, and colleagues will be far more harsh and direct than your professors in giving their feedback. In most large companies or organizations, no letter or document goes out until it has been edited and re-edited at several levels to avoid including anything remotely unprofessional.

Progressive organizations can also be very rewarding to those who possess good writing skills. Really good writers, like really good thinkers, are increasingly rare commodities. Good writing skills can take you far in your chosen profession.

COMMON SPELLING ERRORS

Some spelling mistakes are made much more often than others. Remember the following:

- Compliment means to say something nice. He paid me a *compliment* about my report.
- Complement means to fit together. Her work *complements* my work.
- Principle (noun) refers to a rule. A *principle* of the legal system is the right to a lawyer.
- Principal (adjective) means most important. The *principal* character in the play is the mother.
- Principal (noun) is a person in a position of leadership. A *principal* heads the school.
- Affect (usually a verb) means to influence. My gender *affected* my chances.
- Effect (usually a noun) is a result or consequence. The *effect* of the treatment was successful.
- Effect (sometimes a verb) means to bring about. I will *effect* a change in my life.

Lab reports and similar assignments

Although the above sections deal primarily with essays, many of their comments apply to other types of writing that you may do in university, whether they be book reviews, journals, or case studies.

A lab report is something of an exception, however. It is fairly restrictive and formulaic, so be sure that you know exactly what is required and don't deviate from it.

Case studies are more concise and business-like in style and have an organization all their own. They move rapidly from description and analysis to an optimal solution. However, they do leave room to explore alternatives and to demonstrate critical and even creative thinking.

The last word

This chapter has provided specific tools and suggestions for bettering your performance on exams and written assignments. You can also use them to improve many areas of your schoolwork that need attention. However, remember that you need time to develop a style or method that works best for you and gives the results you desire. The more you hone your style or method during your university days, the more you can expect it to serve you well after graduation.

Just as Disneyland wasn't built overnight, becoming a good writer takes time. But in the workplace, there are few skills that have a bigger payoff than the ability to express complex thoughts in written form.

CHAPTER 4

Strengthening Your Critical Skills

> By three methods we may learn wisdom: first, by reflection,
> which is noblest; second, by imitation, which is easiest; and
> third by experience, which is the bitterest.
>
> — Confucius

odern organizations, no matter what their size, need employees who can do more than competently carry out their duties. They need team players who can share, filter, and process information effectively. The kind of skills that you should be acquiring at university and that are key to long-term success at work are known as critical skills. Any progressive employer will want both critical and professional skills.

The primary vehicles for organizing knowledge critically are *concepts* and *theories*. Concepts are the building blocks of theories, and theories are abstract frameworks for understanding data. Together, they provide powerful tools for discovering meaning. Classical economics employs the theory of markets. The key conceptual building blocks of this theory are self-interest, competition, private property, profits, and laissez-faire.

Concepts and theories come in many shapes and sizes, and like the world we live in, they are constantly changing. Being able to adopt and adapt them makes the difference between a merely average student or professional and a really good one. So mastering them is well worth the time and effort.

But we are getting a bit ahead of ourselves here. Before delving more deeply into concepts and theories, we need to get a better handle on the critical skills that your professors and future employers take so seriously.

What are critical skills?

Don't be misled by terminology. Some students seem to think that having critical skills means always criticizing things. Nothing could be further from the truth! In fact, critical skills could just as validly be called *constructive* skills, though of course they also involve *deconstruction* – taking outmoded structures apart.

One sure sign of intellectual immaturity is the tendency to criticize without being willing to reconstruct. Your professors will probably be more tolerant of negativity than your employers because they know how necessary, yet unfamiliar, it is for students to question received knowledge and assumptions. But ultimately, critical thinking must be constructive and strategic if it is to be of any professional use. The slogan "if you're not part of the solution, you're part of the problem" applies to critical skills.

Critical skills are the tools and strategies that we use to creatively analyze, compare, synthesize, and communicate information to resolve confusion and solve problems. These skills are prized in every society, but they are essential in modern life, where intelligent and imaginative thinking are the keys to progress and success. The primary purpose of a university education is to cultivate these skills in future leaders, professionals, and citizens.

Your university studies are designed to build disciplinary and professional, as well as critical, skills. Of the three, however, critical skills are the most important for lifelong learning because they transfer to the widest range of activities. Scholarly disciplines and professional requirements change all the time. Concepts and theories are also subject to change. But the critical skills required to organize concepts in relation to theories remain constant and apply to all environments. Professional and disciplinary competencies provide you with an entry-level job, but your success in that job and beyond depends on critical skills.

Critical skills are essential to human and organizational flourishing. They allow us to

▶ identify problems and reach intelligent decisions
▶ make connections and create hypotheses to resolve confusion
▶ compare and contrast the implications of particular strategies
▶ evaluate and communicate a preferred outcome
▶ act confidently and decisively.

Communication and critical thinking

Problem solving is the heart of critical thinking, but communication is its soul. It's so important that we'll explore the connection between communicative and critical skills right here and delay talking about problem solving until Chapters 7 and 8.

If you can't communicate clearly, you can't think critically. Sounds a bit harsh, doesn't it? Students occasionally complain to us, especially when they get a low mark on an essay or presentation, that they're being treated unfairly. But when we go over their assignment critically and constructively, it usually turns out that they didn't apply critical thinking and thus didn't understand the content very well.

Good communication skills make for good critical thinking because they provide students and employees with the tools to define and solve problems with clarity. Communication, especially in the form of dialogue or debate with others, has been regarded as a chief catalyst for thinking at least since the days of the ancient Greeks. With the invention of paper, writing became the primary medium for developing and conveying critical skills. This is why essay writing remains such a fundamental part of a university education.

One reason why universities and employers hold critical and communication skills in such high esteem is that these skills are not easy to cultivate. We humans are an amazingly intelligent species, but we can also be mentally lazy, suggestible, emotional, habitual, and prejudiced creatures. Not only do we need to work hard to cultivate our critical skills, but we must also work even harder to apply them consistently and continually. The phrase "use it or lose it" applies to critical skills.

Do you know why people with advanced university degrees don't get Alzheimer's as often or as early as the general population?

It's certainly not because they are genetically superior. It's because they typically work in professions or for organizations that require them to practise communicative and critical skills.

Students often assume that communication just means talking to others and, hopefully, managing to entertain, interest, or convince them. Inexperienced students often make the mistake of trying to communicate information in ways that they hope will please their professor. What they fail to understand is that communication does not take place solely with respect to other people. Learning to think critically involves *communicating with ourselves.*

We do this all the time, but our self-communication typically has a lot of static and is full of misleading or contradictory meanings. When we talk to ourselves, our habits or feelings usually get in the way of real understanding. Critical thinking is the method for eliminating static and communicating more meaningfully with ourselves. The most successful people in any profession, and in life generally, are those who have learned to do this.

Communication relates to critical thinking in three fundamental ways:

1 Communication skills allow you to clearly *identify* a problem; if you can achieve this, you're already well on the way to solving it.

2 Words are symbols. They stand for something. The better you are at using them to communicate, the more deeply you can *probe* a problem, dilemma, or question.

3 Communication skills are needed to *connect* symbols or concepts to theories. Concepts are the building blocks of theories, and theories are the most sophisticated ways of organizing knowledge.

Most people have a superficial approach to problems; they tend to believe what they're told or whatever is easiest to understand. Because they lack the capacity to symbolize effectively, most jump too quickly to simplistic solutions that are a dime a dozen. Their loss is your gain. By developing your critical skills, you can set yourself apart and provide value-added information and analysis at school and at work.

Strengthening your critical skills

Nobody ever said that developing critical skills was easy. If it were, critical thinkers wouldn't be in such high demand. But many writers on critical skills make things more difficult than they have to be by throwing tons of abstract stuff at you and hoping that some of it will stick. A better approach is to begin by recognizing that you've always been able to think critically; you just didn't know how to focus this skill until now. The trick is to rigorously and systematically practise the thought processes that you've performed intuitively in the past.

Our goal in this chapter is to reveal some of the invisible rules behind critical skills, so that you can apply them for yourself. But before you begin this journey, consider a tried-and-true piece of advice: almost no one learns critical skills by trying to memorize all the rules. As Michael Gilbert suggests,

> Like trying to remember someone's name, the harder you try, the more difficult it becomes; but, as soon as you give up, relax, and stop trying, the name comes to mind ... The information is there, you have been accumulating it; by *relaxing and listening,* you allow the mind to react freely to what is heard. A similar situation exists in sports. You can learn all there is to know about the correct tennis or golf swing, but *thinking* about your right arm while on the court or links is the worst thing you can do. Instead, a coach will recommend you relax completely and clear your mind.[6]

Learning critical skills is like learning a professional sport; it is difficult, but that doesn't mean it has to be unpleasant. There are few things in life that give as much satisfaction as solving a mental problem. Really nailing the argument in an essay or composing an effective report is a lot like making a great golf shot or scoring a goal. Making sense of a complex issue that you might once have considered beyond your skill is like finally pulling off a hat trick on home ice.

The most important critical skill is the ability to *identify key concepts and ideas.* Far too many students and employees are passive. In learning situations, they behave like open vessels that expect to be filled. Because of this, they have trouble sorting out the key ideas from everything else. When thinking critically, you must separate the important concepts from the examples or the evidence used to support them.

You use concepts all the time, probably without realizing it. Concepts are symbolic tools that are designed to aid understanding. They don't come out of the air. They are cultural inventions. The concept of adolescence, for example, was created during the nineteenth century; before that time, teenagers simply didn't exist. The concept of the peer group was invented in the twentieth century by social scientists. The term "globalization" was unknown thirty years ago. Social media, cyberspace, and much else that is central to our lives and world have an even shorter history.

"Peer group" is a concept or symbol that has a definition, and though dictionary and encyclopedia definitions are useful, they are usually limited. A complex body of scholarly and professional information on peer groups has made the concept more analytically useable. You probably have an intuitive understanding of your own peer group, but do you know all of its characteristics? Demographers, marketers, teachers, actuaries, criminologists, and many other professions have *unpacked* the peer group concept in fascinating ways. For example, advertisers and marketers try to manipulate your insecurities and your need to simultaneously belong to, but stand out from, the crowd.

Concepts are rarely employed in isolation. To make them more useable, scientists tend to organize them in clusters and to distinguish between the ones that are fundamental (sometimes called independent variables) and those that are more secondary (sometimes called dependent variables). What is fundamental and what is secondary usually depends on the particular issue or problem at hand. Thus, we may be trying to understand peer group pressure as a dependent variable of adolescence, or we may be researching adolescence as just one part of life in which peer pressure occurs. Other forms of peer pressure might arise in crowds, religious cults, suburban environments (keeping up with the Joneses), and elsewhere.

Concept clusters can range from the relatively simple to the much more complex. Concepts in the academic disciplines, for example, tend to be organized within sophisticated classificatory systems. You may think that you already know what is meant by a concept such as democracy. But we guarantee that you'll have a much more sophisticated understanding of that concept cluster if you take a course in political science. For example, the concept cluster of democracy has at least three quite separate dimensions:

▷ free elections in which everyone has a vote
▷ freedom of expression and association
▷ a government controlled by an elected legislature.

Within and between these three dimensions, there are many different variations that political scientists study. Indeed, defining democracy is the topic of entire university courses and many books.

You might notice that the definition of democracy presented above doesn't say anything about free enterprise or capitalism, something that people often associate with democracy. Concept clusters invariably make *assumptions* and often exhibit distinctive *biases*. But some assumptions and biases may be necessary to make the concepts work, whereas others could be entirely unwarranted. A genuinely democratic society, for example, need not be capitalistic: it could just as easily be socialist or communist.

The limitations of narrative

Human communities have always organized and passed on significant information in the form of *narratives*, or stories. There is nothing wrong with this: narratives are both valuable ways of knowing and important sources of information. They are essential to personal and cultural identity. But using narrative to construct knowledge does have some serious limitations.

Younger students often try to make information meaningful by organizing it within a narrative. When writing a research paper, they can be very good at providing a basic plot, and they often try to add value by giving lots of details. But relatively few beginners are good at dissecting and illuminating the fundamental *meaning* or *significance* of the story.

Most of our students enjoy movies, so we often mention them when we teach critical skills. You can watch a movie superficially, in terms of its plot, or you can watch it critically. A good film should communicate meanings. At least some of its meanings will be invisible to anyone who simply wants to be entertained with a lively plot. A truly great and lasting film will challenge your assumptions by providing subtle and complex meanings. If you are accustomed to thinking critically, a movie that relies solely on a romantic or clever story line may seem to insult your intelligence.

Take, for example, the movie *Pretty Woman*, starring Julia Roberts and Richard Gere. Though admittedly well-acted and moderately enjoyable, it's relatively *meaningless* because it doesn't convey very deep or interesting messages. It trots out some trite beliefs, such as the idea that love conquers all, that every woman will find her Mr. Right, and that all of us have an equal shot at happiness. This combination becomes remotely plausible only for those who look like Julia Roberts and have the good fortune to acquire a benefactor who is also a millionaire. Moreover, most millionaires tend to look more like Bill Gates or Donald Trump than Richard Gere.

When we say things like this, our students sometimes complain that we are being too cynical. They legitimately argue that most movies are pleasant stories, fantasies that ask us to suspend our disbelief. That's fine as far as it goes, and at least it shows some degree of critical separation. But many people internalize the fantasies and make very poor marital and career choices as a result. Some even feel like failures when their lives don't measure up to the movies. They often lack the critical skills to cope effectively with reality.

Lots of our students don't initially perceive that most Hollywood movies are no more than superficial entertainment. The plot of *Pretty Woman* is loosely based on a play by George Bernard Shaw (1856-1950) called *Pygmalion*. Shaw's play offers much more sophisticated and ambiguous meanings. One of these is that romantic illusions are not necessarily fulfilled and may even be ideological because they mask or excuse some fundamental social problems. Furthermore, he argues that economic and educational inequalities must be seriously addressed if the phrase "equality of opportunity" is to mean anything. You don't necessarily have to agree with Shaw to recognize that he provides some worthwhile food for thought.

What is most *critical* to critical thinking is locating the key concepts and assumptions, and recognizing in advance that they may be both complex and multiple. This means that you must be prepared to work at and dig deeply into the material to find the nuggets that may not be immediately apparent. Not all material contains nuggets. *Pretty Woman*, for instance, has little to offer beyond passive entertainment. But you can bet that your university-level readings and assignments will.

Being critical means recognizing and assessing various levels of meaning. True critical thinkers can list the best movies and explain the reasons for their choice. Almost all film critics, for example, think that *Citizen Kane* (1941) is one of the greatest American movies ever made. Why? Because the movie – directed, co-written, produced by, and starring Orson Welles (1915-1985) – delivers many levels of meaning. It's based on the story of William Randolph Hearst (1863-1951), a rich American newspaper publisher. It's also a moral drama that shows us how power and wealth can corrupt. It's an allegory on the rise of the American nation, from innocence to complicity. It's a study in ambiguity that illuminates the complexities of a human being rather than giving a black-and-white stereotype. Finally, it's an artistic masterpiece that uses metaphors in a sophisticated way to deliver complex messages.

The more closely you concentrate on *Citizen Kane*, the more you get from it. In fact, most people miss at least some of its meaning the first time around. The latest Hollywood or Bollywood blockbuster may provide more entertainment value than *Citizen Kane*, but there is no comparison in terms of depth, technique, and significance.

Contextualizing information

Being able to identify key concepts and ideas is important, but you also need to compare and contextualize them. In the original play *Peter Pan* by J.M. Barrie (1860-1937) and in various movie adaptations, we are presented with certain key ideas:

1 The creative imagination is important.
2 People are inherently good, and childhood is a period of innocence and imaginative potential.
3 Adults need to retain their childlike qualities.
4 Children need to grow up and take responsibility for their actions.

In the 1904 play *Peter Pan*, the key idea or primary message is number four. In the 1991 movie *Hook*, the key idea is number three. In the 2004 movie *Finding Neverland*, the key meaning is number two. This shift in focus makes for very different emphases and meaning, even though the basic plot remains recognizable.

The difference between *Peter Pan* the play and the movies *Hook* and *Finding Neverland* leads us into a very important component of critical skills – assessing the context of the information. Key ideas and concepts are *foreground* information, but we often need to take the *background* into account if we wish to uncover them.

The background can exist in various forms. In the case of *Peter Pan*, we might want to examine the author's intention. Barrie was a Scotsman who lived at a time when the British Empire was at its height, and the ideal values of society were patriarchal and military. He might have seen childhood as a wonderful and formative period (the place where moral ideas are constructed), but he probably believed that adults (particularly men) needed to take responsibility for themselves and take an active role in governing an extensive empire. There was a time to be a child and a time to grow up.

Hook was produced during a very different historical period. In the 1990s, many Americans felt that their lives were becoming bureaucratic, materialistic, and dissatisfying. They yearned for a return to the ostensibly innocent values of rural America (as interpreted by Walt Disney). Thus, *Hook*'s Peter Pan , now a corporate lawyer and a complete failure as a human being, rediscovers his childlike innocence and imagination. The settings and characters of *Hook* are essentially the same as in the Barrie play, but its primary message or meaning could not be more different. *Finding Neverland*, made not long after the 9/11 bombings, emphasizes the role of friendships and family, and the goodness that comes from relationships.

Context includes many things that can give clues to meaning. These can include the date when something was composed (history), the style in which it is written (literary genre or scientific paradigm), and what we know about the author's life (biography) and socio-political position.

Exploring context is just one way of determining meaning and can sometimes be misleading. Besides, it often limits our understanding of and appreciation for a given issue or work. One of the most important clues to meaning lies in the use of *symbols*. These convey complex, subtle, or ambiguous meanings and are typically more common in literary works than in social scientific writing. Although they are certainly not lacking in the social sciences, the requirements of systematic analysis tend to limit their use. In works that rely more on imagination, symbols function as metaphors.

In her novel *To the Lighthouse*, for example, Virginia Woolf (1882-1941) continually refers to various types of ocean waves. Sometimes the waves are mere ripples, and all seems secure and serene. Sometimes they are choppy and distinct from each other. At one point, they beat viciously against the shore. To understand their significance, you need to think in symbolic terms, using your critical skills to recognize that the waves have more to do with the novel's meaning than with its plot. The waves stand for human relationships. Human beings are connected with each other in the social ocean. But waves also connote the isolation that divides individuals. Consequently, human beings are sometimes connected with one another and sometimes apart. Occasionally, they clash (as in the First World War, which appears in the book) and the human community is transformed into a stormy and threatening ocean.

Thus, the symbol of the waves reveals meaning in *To the Lighthouse*. If you paid attention to them, you'd have a much better understanding of what this great work of literature is about. This is particularly true because it focuses so intently on the interior world of its characters that the plot sometimes seems insignificant.

In great works that employ a more traditional narrative approach, you can still find an attention to symbols. In *Citizen Kane*, for example, the protagonist's (main character) dying word is "rosebud." If you watch the movie closely, you'll discover that Rosebud was the name painted on his sleigh, when he was a young child and full of promise.

To discover the meaning of any book, article, essay, or work of art, it is important to focus on the title. Literary authors often use key symbols in their titles. One of Virginia Woolf's other novels is simply called *The Waves*. The title of Sylvia Plath's (1932-63) novel *The Bell Jar* tells a lot about the message that she wanted to convey. A bell jar is an inverted glass dome that scientists use to measure how long mice or insects take to use up the oxygen in a confined space. Plath's novel is about a highly intelligent woman who lives in a society where women are not allowed to develop their own identities and often end up in stifling relationships with men. See the connection? Why do you think Plath is such an inspiration to feminist writers?

Important symbols appear in even the most seemingly scientific works. Nicolaus Copernicus (1473-1543) referred to the Greek image of a lantern in the centre of the sky to help readers reimagine a world where the planets revolved around the sun. To assist his readers in visualizing the workings of the free market (where supply and demand are in equilibrium), Adam Smith (1723-90) used the image, or metaphor, of an invisible or hidden hand. This symbolized the idea that supply and demand would naturally balance each other only if the government refrained from meddling in the market.

Smith needed the support of this symbol because in 1776, when he wrote *The Wealth of Nations*, virtually no one had dreamed of a free market, and most people had difficulty in picturing one. Once a symbol is used, it can be adopted by others. Many economists view the hidden hand as Smith's primary meaning for their discipline, whereas he himself might have used it merely to support his preference for less-regulated markets. To understand what Smith was saying, therefore, you might need to take both his symbol and his context into account.

You might also want to recognize that writers sometimes rework or even invert symbols. The modern economic historian Alfred Chandler (1918-2007) played on Smith's symbol in the title of his book *The Visible Hand*. What do you think it was about? How does the modern economy work? Who has the power to direct or manipulate the market? Chandler's message is that we no longer operate in a free marketplace: global corporations increasingly control our lives and the risks of the market.

The significance of theories

Alfred Chandler had a *point of view*. He thought that modern corporations are too big and powerful. Adam Smith had a point of view. He believed that progress was possible only if capitalists were forced to compete in the marketplace without too much government interference. Virginia Woolf wanted to advise her readers to appreciate the moment and enjoy the little pleasures of life, because these were the most human and tangible things that could be experienced in a confusing and occasionally chaotic world. Sylvia Plath also had a perspective, or point of view. She was a feminist writer in some important respects, even if she would probably have rejected the label "feminist." She believed that intelligent women were suffocated in a male-dominated society.

A point of view, or perspective, is a *theory*. There's nothing intrinsically mysterious about theories. They are just useful abstractions that combine, organize, and distinguish related concepts for explanatory purposes. In fact, you use theories all the time. If you think that Bill Gates must be smart because he's so rich, you are invoking a theory (however dubious) that all wealthy people are intelligent. Same thing when you say, "If you're so smart, how come you're not rich?" The data may not necessarily support your theory, however.

An academic theory is very careful about how it uses data (facts) and formulates claims about them. Scholars are expected to be scrupulous in processing information, to limit their claims to what the data support, and to continually test their abstractions against the available evidence. Usually, they apply the word "theory" only to highly integrated, tightly argued, and logically warranted explanations.

The theories used in the liberal arts (the social sciences and humanities) commonly differ from those of the physical sciences (chemistry, physics, and related). In the physical sciences, many theories, though not all or even the most important ones, *predict* an outcome, whereas in the liberal arts, they tend to be more *explanatory*. But these differences are less important than what theories have in common. In essence, they all attempt to discover the primary or important causes for certain events or outcomes. In other words, they try to make sense of a bunch of material that would otherwise be much less comprehensible or useful.

Acquiring critical skills means thinking not only more deeply but also more expertly. Demonstrating expertise implies having a bag of tools or techniques that will help you mine more deeply and probe for diamonds. The most valuable tools for probing data are *theoretical* approaches or *frameworks*. Many of these are available in academic disciplines or the professions. Let's say, for example, that you want to understand how critical skills usually develop among your fellow university students. To achieve this, you might want to adopt a theoretical framework developed by Benjamin Bloom. Bloom's theory goes like this:

1 First-year university students tend to see the world in black and white. They want their teachers to tell them what's right and wrong. They take in information passively and uncritically.

2 In second year, students begin to realize that the operative word is "grey" rather than "black and white." At this point, they know that meanings are multiple and that facts need to be interpreted. However, though they understand that viewpoints are significant, they are not very adept at handling theoretical frameworks. They tend to think that they (and everyone else) are entitled to their opinion.

3 In third year, students begin to use theoretical frameworks more adroitly and learn to back up their arguments logically and with evidence. However, they probably still lack a coherent world of personal meaning with which to process the information that they receive. They have learned to think more critically but are still dependent on their teachers.

4 With a little luck, fourth-year students will develop theoretical frameworks of their own, which they apply *independently* in their studies. They recognize diversity but can form and integrate material for themselves. In dealing with texts and other material, they no longer lean on the opinions and approaches of their professors.[7]

Bloom's four-part progression is not a dogmatic account of how students develop but a theoretical framework for understanding mental, personal, and ethical growth.

Theories are systematic ways of interpreting or making sense of reality. Although they have explanatory or predictive power, they rarely claim the status of absolute truths, even in fields such as physics and chemistry. Rather, they are useful ways of organizing complex material. Not every first-year student will conform to Bloom's stereotype. And not every fourth-year student will be as mature and independent as he hopes.

Just because theories are important tools doesn't make them immune to critical analysis. Feminist scholars, for example, have criticized Bloom's model for its gendered one-sidedness. They suggest that though it measures male development fairly well, it's not so good at describing female psychological development and maturity. Can you guess how a feminist scholar might criticize Bloom's model? Can you think of a different one, or even variations of his model? If so, you are already demonstrating a capacity for critical thinking.

Theoretical levels and forms

Theoretical frameworks take a variety of forms and operate on a number of levels. To put it simply, some are meta theories – big, overarching constructs that explain huge chunks of reality. Others are micro theories, which explain small, local phenomena. And some operate at the meso level, commonly forming a link between meta and micro theories. People tend to think in terms of either big or small theories. But they sometimes use a meso-level theory to explain an oddity or a problem in a meta-level theory.

Are you getting lost? Here's an example. A key meta theory from the work of Karl Marx (1818-83) states that the working class (those who are employed by others) will rise in a revolutionary conflict with those who own the means of production and wealth (the employers). If you want to retain the theory but explain why this type of revolution did not occur during the twentieth century, you might want to use a meso theory. This could explain that the revolution was short-circuited by employers and governments, who used rewards (such as higher pay, public health care, and unemployment insurance) and controls (surveillance and threats of outsourcing) to prevent workers from organizing and overthrowing their oppressors.

Bloom's model of student development is a fairly low-level (micro) theory that is an adaptation of a meta theory created by the psychologist Jean Piaget (1896-1980). In the liberal arts and social sciences, large, overarching meta theories are extremely important and fundamental ways of organizing knowledge and understanding data. Some examples of meta theories include Marxism, Freudianism, feminism, existentialism, pragmatism, deconstruction, and postmodernism. There are lots more. These *really big* theories often incorporate many aspects of human existence, such as psychology, spirituality, economics, philosophy, sociology, and ethics. Sometimes they are compatible with each other; more often they are mutually exclusive.

Meta theories will always be popular and have a *cool* factor because they provide considerable explanatory power and can completely transform the way in which we look at data or reality (they're often counterintuitive). Plus, applying them well takes a hell of a lot of critical skill.

Some scholars spend their entire working lives exploring Sigmund Freud's (1856-1939) theory of the id, ego, and superego. Many Marxist academics continue to refine and update Marx's theory of dialectical materialism. There's even a school of Jacques Derrida (1930-2004) scholars in literature departments who will try to convince you that there's no such thing as an author – only abandoned texts that leave differential traces of meaning.

You are not expected to become experts in these theories during your undergraduate years. But learning to think critically will involve absorbing some concepts and approaches from the various theories because they are such useful tools. For example, Karl Marx suggested that human history should be understood as the conflict between social classes. If you use this theoretical approach, you'll be able to make sense of many historical events, such as wars, revolutions, strikes, protests, bombings, and so on.

Sigmund Freud illuminated the power of the subconscious. You will find lots of evidence of his influence in modern novels and in

FOUR MAJOR THEORIES OF SOCIOLOGY

Every field or academic discipline has certain favourite theories. Below, we outline four important examples from sociology, flagging the key concepts with italics.

Structural functionalism: This meta theory states that society is a complex *system,* one composed of many *structures,* such as the family, school, government, and employers, each with a specific *function* that achieves *consensual equilibrium.*

Translation: Modern society is both fair and efficient.

Conflict theory: This meta theory sees society as a fundamentally *unjust* and *unequal* combination of *classes* with *opposing interests,* where the dominant class *exploits* the *labour* of others.

Translation: Modern society is unfair for most people and is ultimately dysfunctional.

Exchange theory: This micro theory suggests that all human interactions have an *economic character* in that people operate on the basis of *self-interest* to obtain *rewards,* including *approval* and affection.

Translation: Everyone is out for him- or herself, and life is a process of negotiation.

Symbolic interactionism: This micro theory holds that people construct their *self* and create *meanings* by interacting with each other, including role playing and using symbols (primarily but not exclusively language).

Translation: Who we are is determined solely by our interaction with others – family, friends, teachers.

movies such as *Memento,* which use techniques such as stream of consciousness and mental flashbacks to explore the mind. You don't need a perfect understanding of existentialism or of Jean-Paul Sartre's complex discussion of consciousness to appreciate some of his insights into our modern crises of meaning. Everyone who has made difficult ethical choices, or observed the many hypocritical ways in which we excuse our selfish behaviour, or ever felt that "hell is other people" can take something from the existentialist canon (body of theories).

At this point, you might be wondering what any of this has to do with life after university. If so, you haven't fully grasped the enormous power of critical thinking. At the minimum, simply being able to work confidently with theories implies that you can detach yourself from the increasing and overwhelming flow of information and form useful abstractions. A theoretical facility will make you a much more effective sifter and processor of information in an age when these skills are the most essential. Even if you don't accept every aspect of a certain theory, you will often find that parts of it are indispensable.

Big theories will seem irrelevant if you don't know how, when, and where to apply some of their tools. For instance, Sartre can tell our corporate executives a lot about why they should accept responsibility for their decisions. He can also show corporate critics how some executives habitually practise bad faith with shareholders and stakeholders. Max Weber's (1864-1920) theories about large organizations and Freud's analysis of civilization can help someone in a human resources department understand why employees become unhappy in unnecessarily bureaucratic and rule-bound situations, and why workplaces might need to pay more attention to their mental health. Marx is indispensable to anyone who wants to discover why employees distrust their bosses and feel alienated at work. Even someone as esoteric as Derrida, when taught properly and with a minimum of jargon, can assist those who work in global and multicultural environments to reach beyond their Eurocentric perspective and learn to respect and embrace cultural diversity.

The significant differences and incompatibilities between some major theoretical perspectives often frustrate beginning students, who want to know "which one is right." These differences, however, can be real advantages for anyone who is interested in the practical use of theories. Applying various theoretical perspectives to a problem is an extremely effective way of discovering interesting angles, strategic possibilities, and novel solutions. You can use a theory to clarify issues and solve problems without subscribing to the entire package.

Just remind yourself that no single theoretical perspective can ever completely capture the complexities of human life and relationships. The world and any given individual are too multifaceted to be explained by just one theory. Indeed, this complexity suggests that multiple perspectives are necessary to understand our environment and ourselves. People who use a single theoretical approach to make sense of everything may seem deep, but they are often inflexible and one-dimensional.

Even if you don't have many opportunities to formally use meta theories after you graduate, you can transfer the interpretive facility and depth of thinking that goes with them to any profession. The stronger your critical skills, the more employable and successful you will be. There is no question, however, that you'll need to be familiar with the meta and micro theories that are relevant in your occupation.

During the past forty years, business managers have had to learn many new theories as part of running a company. In fact, it's difficult to think of any really challenging future occupation in which success won't depend on continually updating knowledge. This also entails keeping abreast of the latest theoretical approaches in a profession or occupation.

That's why it is important to begin blending theory and practice now. Look for opportunities to relate the latest theories to practical issues in the real world: these could include business and political ethics, the impact of technology, the influence of globalization, the meaning of love, and much, much more. Graduates who take their theoretical know-how to the workplace, and keep it fresh with advances in the field, are real assets to their employers.

Your university instructors don't expect to transform you into abstract theoreticians (though it may occasionally seem that way). We'll let you in on a little secret – even professors can have a hard time keeping up with new theories. But we'll also guarantee that, with practice, you'll become increasingly adept at deploying them in combination or tailoring them to specific situations and problems.

Practical tips to help you on your way

Some people naively believe that intelligence is something that we're born with (or not) and place far too much emphasis on IQ and GPA scores. We've got good news for anyone who has ever felt stupid. True intelligence consists of applying critical skills. What's more, the skills can be learned! If you read this chapter carefully, you are already well on the way to developing them.

Here's a little test. Can you tell why *Blade Runner, 2001: A Space Odyssey*, or even *The Matrix* (the original, not the sequels) are better than the *Star Wars* movies? Can you tell why the Beatles' *Sgt. Pepper* album or Radiohead's *OK Computer* are more meaningful than anything by the Kid Ink, Justin Bieber, or Britney Spears? To understand and be able to explain the difference is critical thinking. It doesn't mean that you have to *like* the Beatles better than Bieber. All that's expected is that, as you develop your critical taste, you'll learn to distinguish and appreciate more sophisticated and more deeply layered material.

Acquiring critical skills doesn't happen overnight. It is a gradual learning process. That's why an undergraduate program typically takes at least four years; it's designed to develop your critical skills. Too many university teachers, however, seem to believe that students will pick them up simply by osmosis. If they hang around long enough, they'll begin to *cotton on*. But your approach can be much more proactive and systematic than this.

The first step is to begin *making connections* between what you already know and what you are encountering in school. Everybody starts from somewhere, and personal experience is the smartest place to begin. When you explore new material, one of the best things you can do is to *engage* with it. What does it mean to you? Do you agree with it? If yes, why? If no, why not? You will understand and appreciate more sophisticated materials better if you can relate to them in some way.

But that's just a starting point. Too many students are daunted by sophisticated material because they find it difficult, foreign, and challenging. Their natural tendency is to oversimplify it to make themselves feel comfortable or reject it because it differs from what they've seen before. In such situations, it's absolutely crucial

A NOTE ON JARGON

Don't be spooked by jargon. It's only words. You already use tons of jargon when speaking with your friends. The purpose of academic jargon is to allow scholars to condense a lot of ideas or complex concepts into a single word or phrase. Terms such as sexism, bureaucracy, hegemony, social class, ideology, cognitive dissonance, hegemony, Protestant ethic, peer pressure, and even something as commonly used as "culture" were invented by social scientists or liberal arts scholars to communicate ideas more effectively. And let's be honest, using jargon correctly makes you a member of a special club.

to *suspend judgment* and explore the material as fully as possible. Your professor will give you study material that is rich in symbols and meanings. If you reject it in an offhand manner because it's unfamiliar or intimidating, you impose unnecessary barriers to learning. To develop your critical skills, you'll need to do a lot of work up front. You are like a miner. If you simply extract information, it is like mining for coal – useful but not very profitable. If you hunt for concepts and deeper meanings in the coal, your chances of finding a diamond (crystallized coal) are considerable.

Working with theories can seem difficult, but they were designed by some of the world's smartest intellectual engineers and are the best mining tools we have. Don't expect theoretical arguments to read like magazine articles: their purpose is not to entertain but to analyze and instruct. Don't be put off by the technical jargon either.

Gradually, as your critical skills develop, all of this will seem less difficult, and your enjoyment in creating meaningful knowledge will make your work a lot more pleasurable. The thinking process that appears so difficult now will become second nature. You will find yourself discovering all sorts of things that a critical intelligence has the ability to reveal. The indispensable first step is to suspend judgment and engage in exploration. The results will be worth it.

Developing critical skills is more like running a marathon than a hundred-yard dash. Persistence and practice really do pay off. Unlike most physical skills, however, critical skills can be practised throughout your life and will enrich it immeasurably.

CHAPTER 5
Active Listening and Active Reading

> Reading is thinking with someone else's head instead of
> one's own.
>
> — Arthur Schopenhauer

It's fascinating to watch students before a lecture. As they file into the room, they're laughing, chatting, and discussing a recent date or last night's show. They are energized, bursting with vitality, and brimming with personal opinions. Then the instructor comes in, the lecture begins, and the students pick up their computers or pens and furiously begin to write notes that are basically lists of factual information. In the blink of an eye, most students are transformed from active and involved human beings into passive recipients of an external body of knowledge. This inclination to gravitate toward *passive listening and learning* is the single biggest obstacle to developing critical skills.

The lecturing process has been described as the transfer of the speaker's notes to the listener's notebook without any achievement of understanding in the minds of either. Although this is a stereotype, it does highlight the tendency of lectures to encourage passive learning that leads to passive study habits. To get the most from a lecture, you need to actively listen and engage with the lecturer and material. This means being proactive and taking the initiative – a very different state of mind from passive listening and learning.

Passive listening

When attending a lecture in a passive state of mind, you

▸ expect to be spoon-fed information
▸ want that information to be structured as conveniently as possible to help you on assignments and exams
▸ resist any invitation to think more deeply about a subject, explore ambiguities, or deal with anything that *isn't on the exam*
▸ consider the subject closed once the lecture ends, at least until exam time.

Passivity doesn't mean that you've been totally lobotomized. You can still appreciate the difference between boring and entertaining lectures. You recognize that some professors know their stuff and can convey it better than others. But you don't use the higher forms of thought that involve comparing, analyzing, synthesizing, and evaluating.

When you are in passive mode, it is impossible to digest the material and make it truly your own. Facts stay in your short-term memory and are discarded as soon as you write the final exam. The tragedy is that you'll come away with nothing more than a grade.

Active listening

Active listening differs entirely from passive listening because it involves

▸ being attentive to what is said, how it is said, what is repeated, and what is underlined
▸ seeking connections between what you already know and what is being said
▸ focusing on the key ideas that allow you to organize the facts
▸ engaging in a mental dialogue with the lecturer
▸ identifying his or her perspective or theoretical approach
▸ being aware of possible counter-positions
▸ keeping complex ideas in mind for further reflection
▸ making notes of ideas that are unclear.

The words that best describe active listening are dialogue, reflection, and creative tension. If any of these are missing, chances are that you are not listening actively.

The first few times that you attempt to listen actively, you'll probably experience equally active resistance from an underused brain that is not accustomed to being worked so forcefully. You'll find it every bit as painful as beginning a strenuous exercise program. Take care not to overdo it.

An effective approach for beginners is to concentrate on just one or two points. The most useful strategy is probably to focus on identifying the things that you don't understand and being pro-active about approaching your professor for clarification during his or her office hours, or conducting further research on your own.

Active listening requires your full attention. Distractions such as a working computer, a nearby smartphone, or even whispering friends make it unattainable. Not surprisingly, it's also easier in the front or middle of a classroom than in the back.

Active reading

Active reading means reading with your complete attention and with focus. In other words, it's about making text meaningful. Written material can have many levels of meaning. Here are a few of the most important ones:

- The *genre:* Is the text a novel, poem, essay, or a work of non-fiction?
- The *context:* In what historical period, physical setting, and kind of society did the writer live?
- The *audience:* Was the text written for women or men, rich or poor, adults or children, the highly educated or a mass audience?
- The *explicit or implicit message:* What is the author trying to say or tending to assume?
- The *levels of meaning:* Does the text operate on a number of levels?
- The *hidden meanings:* What symbols or codes does the writer use to convey special meaning?
- The *unintended meanings:* What meanings can critical readers attribute to the text that the author never intended?

▷ The *attributed meanings:* Has the text been read differently by different groups at different times?

▷ The *academic significance:* What is the significance of the text for the university course in which it is being read?

▷ The *personal meaning* for you: How was the text special for you, or how did it affect you?

You will no doubt have noticed that we left the personal meaning until the end. There's a good reason for this. Many students become far too caught up in their own personal reaction to what they read. Because a complex text has many possible meanings, students often make the mistake of assuming that their own opinions should take pride of place in interpreting it.

Active reading means *suspending* your personal and often emotional response to a text to explore its meanings more thoughtfully, analytically, and synthetically. First impressions, with texts as with people, are often misleading. The more you learn about the various possible meanings of a text, the more you will appreciate the book, essay, or poem.

Reading at an academic level

Not all written material demands the same level of concentration. Spy thrillers and romance novels are mass-market publications for passive consumption. One goal of university education is to develop active and critical reading by exposing you to more demanding forms of literature. Academic thinking and everyday mass media thinking lie at the opposite ends of the intellectual spectrum. The latter is characterized by brief, categorical, and general statements; the former consists of carefully constructed, highly nuanced, and detached hypotheses that are supported by evidence and argument.

A great advantage of critical or active reading is that it allows readers to deconstruct all sorts of writing, to expose stereotypes and prejudices, and to develop clear and independent positions. It also enables readers to discover the manipulative techniques that advertisers use to make us go out and buy their products. For example, scholars who study marketing have exposed the ways in which the fashion industry tries to make women feel dissatisfied with their bodies, often with serious consequences, such as anorexia and bulimia.

Most websites simply cry out for critical reading and listening skills because they are rarely subject to scholarly or specialized scrutiny.

By now it should be clear that active reading is different from memorizing parts of text and that it goes beyond merely describing or summarizing them. The purpose of active reading is to get you to think harder and to go more deeply into the material. It's best to start developing these skills one text at a time. But once your skills improve, you need to go beyond the text to create *networks of meaning*. This is achieved by

▶ *linking* texts to each other
▶ comparing and *evaluating* the various approaches to texts
▶ *integrating* texts with scholarly articles and analyses.

All of this may initially sound very complex and time consuming, but becomes second nature as you hone your active reading skills. In the long run, it's also a much more efficient way of learning than memorization. Because memorization relies on your short-term memory, you will forget most of what you've read within a year.

Active reading produces mental networks of understanding that will stay with you forever. Students who have a photographic memory, but who are not active readers, may have an initial advantage, but they cannot compete with those who have developed their critical reading skills.

Many individuals have excellent critical skills but could nonetheless benefit from a few tips. Here are four steps that can help:

1 *Skim* the title, introduction, conclusion, summary, chapter headings, and index to see what they can tell you about the book.
2 In textbooks especially, *ask yourself* what particular topics a chapter is addressing. Turning statements into questions is an ideal way of seeing what the author is trying to accomplish.
3 Recite the *key ideas* of the book or article and tape yourself.
4 When you *review*, pay particular attention to the ideas that you couldn't articulate clearly.

In addition to the steps outlined above, many critical skills instructors have developed specific reading strategy sheets for various kinds of texts. The example below was developed for fiction and non-fiction by teaching-award-winning professor Jan Rehner at York University (and is included here with her permission).

READING STRATEGY SHEET FOR FICTION AND NON-FICTION

Fiction	Non-fiction
1 The title What associations does the title trigger? Do you have any guesses as to what the work is about?	**The title** Same
2 The author Have you read anything else by this author? What background information or context notes do you have that might indicate particular content or a characteristic style?	**The author** Same
3 Copyright date and place of publication What do you know about the historical period and culture in which this work was first published?	**Copyright date and place of publication** Same
4 Opening paragraphs or a novel's first chapter What are your impressions of the story's opening or the novel's introductory chapter? What have you learned so far, and what do you think might happen next?	**List of subtitles or table of contents** What kind of topics does the author list as central to the text? Do any headings strike you as unusual? Any missing topics that you expected to find?
5 Character checklist Begin listing the names of important characters and the page number where they first appear. Also jot down your initial impressions of each one. As you read on, make a note if they change.	**Opening paragraphs or introductory chapter** What is the author's main thesis or controlling argument? List the stated or implied purposes of the article or book.

6 **Points worth noting as you read**
The following questions and categories may be useful in helping you to respond to the text. Not all will be relevant, but address as many as you can. Don't forget to record the page numbers.

Point of view. Who is telling the story? Is it one of the characters or an all-knowing narrator? Does the point of view change as the plot progresses?

Figurative language. Are there recurring symbols or patterns of imagery? What do they contribute to the overall meaning of the work?

Setting and atmosphere. What is the setting and mood? How do they make you feel?

Turning points. What are the crucial points of action in the plot? Do the characters make any important choices? Do they experience significant insights or reactions? Do any of the main characters change?

Style. Are there any noteworthy patterns in the author's choice of words? Are the sentences short, long, simple, or complex? Does the author use dialogue effectively?

Thematic concerns. Themes in fiction are usually expressed through a combination of character, images, and action. Looking for themes is a way of deciding what the story or novel is about. What are the various themes of the work? List at least two possibilities.

Points worth noting as you read
The following questions and categories may be useful in helping you to respond to the text. Not all will be relevant, but address as many as you can. Don't forget to record the page numbers.

Key terms and definitions. Does the author use italics to stress certain items? Are definitions clear? Jot them down in your own words. Do they match, challenge, or expand your own definitions?

Maps, graphs, and illustrations. If the author uses visual aids, how do they connect to the main thesis or argument?

Quotations and citations. Does the author quote or cite the opinions or published work of experts or other authors? How do these references relate to the main thesis or argument?

Examples and evidence. Does the author clarify abstract ideas by providing concrete examples? Can you illustrate one of the author's ideas with an example of your own? Are the main points supported with convincing evidence? Can you think of any evidence that has been omitted?

Assumptions and biases. Does the author make any statements that can't be proven? Does the author confess to or otherwise reveal any bias that may be shaping the argument?

Figurative language. Are there recurring symbols or patterns of imagery that reinforce the main points?

Style. Are there any noteworthy patterns in the author's choice of words? Are the sentences short, long, simple, or complex?

7 The conclusion	**Concluding paragraphs or summary chapter**
Is the ending satisfying? Is it open to more than one interpretation?	Does the conclusion restate the main thesis? Are you satisfied that the main argument has been well supported? Do the closing remarks supply any related ideas or applications of the argument that might be further explored?
8 Overall impressions and course content What does this work contribute to your knowledge of course issues? What assumptions does the author make about them? How do the author's views compare with those of other authors you have read for the course and outside of it? What assumptions of your own did this story or novel challenge?	**Overall impressions and course content** Same

Perfecting your skills

As you refine your reading skills, your analysis and understanding will become increasingly sophisticated. Here are tips to help guide your progress:

▶ When you begin to read difficult material, it's important to follow logical steps to get a clear understanding. But as your skill develops, you can use the creative, intuitive, and imaginative side of your mind more often. This is sometimes referred to as lateral thinking, and original thinkers do it all the time. But always remember that traditional logical, sequential thinking comes first. Don't try to run before you can walk.

▶ The most interesting problems always have multiple solutions. Once you've learned to read material carefully and critically, you will want to look at it from various perspectives. The best readers are good role-players. As they engage the material, they can imagine themselves as different kinds of readers. Can you put on various hats and imagine how you might respond to a text if you were a young optimist, an older conservative, a corporate executive, a welfare recipient?

▶ You can always apply whatever perspective seems most helpful. You can choose to be provocative, sympathetic, ironic, optimistic, or pessimistic. The only ironclad rule is that you must be clear and fair in your assessment of a reading.

▶ The academic disciplines offer some of the most useful perspectives. The most original thinkers, however, are usually multidisciplinary – they merge various perspectives to discover new ways of looking at material. One such thinker, for example, is Karl Polanyi (1886-1964), who wrote brilliantly on politics and economics. His book *The Great Transformation: The Political and Economic Origins of Our Time* brings together insights from anthropology, history, political science, and economics.

▶ The fact that authors are scientists who follow the rules for scholarship does not necessarily mean that they are unbiased. In fact, everyone is biased in one direction or another. Learning how to detect bias is a good sign that you are becoming a critical reader.

▶ All of us are the products of our own cultures, and they too have certain biases. Your critical reading skills will increase dramatically if you learn to detect and question them. Studying the assumptions of other cultures is also useful here.

▶ Focus as much on what a writer doesn't say as on what he or she does say. Until fairly recently, for example, most writings about business were created by men for men. They reflected a narrow viewpoint and omitted an enormous amount of material. Why have women been so markedly absent from the world of business? Similarly, why do many books on business ignore or disparage the role of workers or trade unions?

Once you gain strong active listening and reading skills, much of what happens in the classroom and the workplace will become more interesting. Even better, your ability to make a valuable contribution will greatly increase.

CHAPTER 6

Researching a Topic

> Nothing in life is to be feared, it is only to be understood. Now is the time to understand more, so that we may fear less.
>
> — Marie Curie

Many manuals on critical skills move directly from active reading to critical writing. The problem with this approach is that it sends the wrong message. Many students make the mistake of transitioning too quickly from reading to writing and then wonder why they get writer's block. Usually, being blocked means that some essential research steps have been omitted.

Sometimes students have a totally impractical approach to writing. They concentrate on the writing process at the expense of the necessary "up front" work. That is, they spend as little time as possible on research, with the intent of giving themselves more time to write. This is the opposite of the way in which an experienced writer works.

Seasoned writers know that research is the most critical part of the process. You should devote roughly 70 percent of your time to research and 30 percent to writing. The writing will flow much better if you've done your research properly. In fact, some writers even say that it takes care of itself if the research is done right. We wouldn't go that far, but it gives you an idea of just how important research is.

Rules of thumb for researchers

The following guidelines will help to improve your research skills:

1 Be curious. You can't do good research unless you are curious about your topic. Being inquisitive helps you to generate the questions or problems that your paper will solve.

2 Identify a subject or topic that interests you. It's difficult to conduct worthwhile research on something that you perceive as dull. The point of doing research is to *satisfy your curiosity*.

3 Use the library (in person or via the Web), databases, course readings, and the Internet to learn what other people have already discovered. To do good research, you need to find good material. Academic research that has been peer reviewed (read critically by scholars before being published) is your best bet. The articles in journals are commonly more useful than books because they are more current and more focused. They do have a few drawbacks, however: they can be highly specialized and written for experts rather than students; their focus can be so narrow that you won't find them useful; they can employ jargon or statistical analyses that are unfamiliar to you.

4 Use books and secondary sources sparingly. Students tend to rely on books, preferably textbooks, for their research. This is because they are familiar with the style and language. Remember, however, that books usually present the research of others and are rarely up to date on the most current issues. Where they can be most useful is in suggesting topics for research, simplifying complex issues, and providing footnotes and bibliographies that can lead you to interesting sources. To be a good researcher, you need to use the academic journals that contain scholarly research.

5 Don't overlook the Internet. The Internet is very useful for facts and data. Therefore, check it for this material but not so much for explanations (that is, for theories and concepts). However, be careful when using popular websites or relying on sites such as

Wikipedia for anything but a starting point in your research. The best sources of data will be books and articles that are accessed through your school library's website. The more you use peer-reviewed scholarly sources, the more sure you can be that the content meets scientific standards.

6 Pay attention to the publication date. The most recent scholarship is often the most relevant. Academic writers usually refer to previous scholarship in their own publications, so you can always work backward from the present if you discover a topic that's worth investigating. There's nothing more irritating than working with material that turns out to be dated.

7 Watch for debates between scholars. These naturally occur in the academic literature, and exploring them can be useful. In most cases, your teachers don't expect you to deal with a topic that has never been discussed before.

8 Identify the problem that you intend to solve or the question that you want to answer. Research is simply organized problem solving. This is so essential that its importance can't be overstated. Trivial problems or questions won't generate interesting essays or answers. Asking rhetorical questions won't reveal anything that's new.

9 Be particularly careful when handling contentious issues. If you chose to explore a highly emotional or controversial topic, you too will need to keep tight rein on your reactions. Be aware of your own bias and aim to write in a balanced manner.

10 Carefully organize and analyze your data. Annotate each article or book that seems useful. An annotation is a four- or five-line summary of a work that reminds you what the author has uncovered and argued. Feel free to add a line or two on your own impressions and any problems and/or contradictions that you discovered in the work.

11 Develop a synopsis of the most important material. A synopsis includes material from several sources (book and articles) and typically consists of several paragraphs. A synopsis is not a summary of a book or articles as with an annotation, but rather deals with

the material as a whole. In doing so, a synopsis includes elements from your critical reading, and takes note of specific details or examples that might help you develop your own argument. Here is an example: "In general, the literature concurs that [two paragraphs]. However, Smith and Jones depart from the norm by suggesting that [one paragraph]. On the whole, the scholarship is weak in dealing with [one paragraph]. Significantly, no one mentions that [one paragraph]."

12 Apply inductive and deductive reasoning to the data. There is no absolute truth in human affairs and no black or white. There are only shades of grey. To make sense of them, we apply various kinds of reasoning. Inductive reasoning means developing generalizations from the facts. Deductive reasoning means using principles or generalizations to organize the facts. In practice, we use both types simultaneously because difficulties can arise when we employ just one or the other.

13 Develop a thesis that you'll apply to the evidence. A thesis can be seen as a *solution to the problem* that you have identified. It will arise from the research that you conduct. Some students believe that coming up with a good thesis or topic involves staring off into space and hoping for a miracle.

14 Draw clear and concise conclusions. Carefully review the results of your research to ensure that they are clear and unambiguous. The whole point of researching is to keep your analysis focused. Aim for depth rather than breadth.

You can solve almost any research problem by narrowing your focus. A common mistake of beginners is picking a topic that is far too broad to address in a university paper, which typically consists of no more than two thousand words. For instance, a subject such as global capitalism is so broad that you can't possibly do justice to it in an essay. Tightening your focus to deal with, say, the economic emergence of Japan after the Second World War will fix the problem.

RESEARCH TIPS

1 Run your topic past your instructor to ensure that it conforms to what is expected. Never presume anything! However, don't ask your professor to suggest a topic. Doing so is a sure sign of passivity.

2 Ask your instructor for suggestions about possible research sources, but never confine yourself to these sources. Show that you are proactive.

3 Many academic disciplines publish summaries, or *abstracts,* of all the articles that appear in peer-reviewed journals each year. Using these abstracts gives quick access to the most useful materials. If you don't know where to find them on-line, ask your university librarian.

4 Skim research first to determine whether it's useful. The last thing you want to do is waste time.

5 Use file cards to make notes and annotations. Use just one card for each reference. That way, you can shuffle cards around.

6 Learn to use reference management software, such as RefWorks. The software will import references from the Internet and apply the desired formatting to your footnotes and bibliography.

7 When creating your research notes, use quotation marks to distinguish between your own paraphrases and material that you copied verbatim from the source. Otherwise, you leave yourself wide open to accusations of plagiarism.

8 Once you've developed a topic or thesis, write it on an index card in bold print and put it over your desk to keep you focused.

9 If you find that an essay needs padding, you haven't done enough research. Go back and do it.

Two research strategies

Anyone can have difficulty in organizing research. You might have a good thesis or topic and even a clear vision of what the paper should ultimately look like. But then, as you decide where things fit and how to organize them most effectively, you run into problems. Some experienced researchers can slot things together in their head, but most of us mere mortals need some help in organizing our thoughts.

The two strategies outlined below will assist in taking ideas from your head and placing them on screen or paper.

RAPID WRITING

Rapid writing is the opposite of normal essay writing. When you compose an essay, you chose your statements carefully with an eye to defending them. In the process, however, some really good intuitive ideas can get lost. Rapid writing is just writing whatever comes to mind about a topic. It's particularly valuable when you've just finished your research and are anxious to begin writing but still don't know how all the pieces fit together.

The rules for rapid writing are simple but important to obey. First, keep it brief. Don't write for more than thirty minutes, or you'll end up trying to compose your essay rather than exploring your research. Second, don't think too hard. Instead, let your intuition and creativity guide you. Third, don't change anything. Fourth, wait until the next day to look at what you wrote, and highlight anything that will be useful for the essay.

MIND MAPPING

The human brain is a weird and wonderful place. It sifts and organizes information in ways that we don't fully understand. The technique of mind mapping approximates the working of the brain at its best.

Here's how to apply it. First, identify the main subject (or thesis) that you want to organize. Put it in the centre of the page or screen.

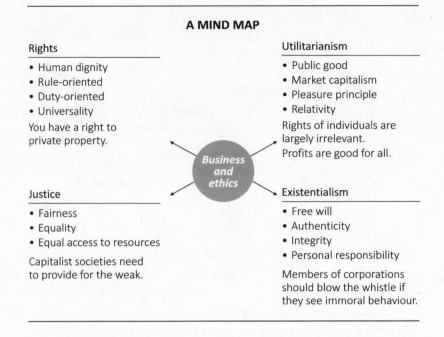

A MIND MAP

Rights

- Human dignity
- Rule-oriented
- Duty-oriented
- Universality

You have a right to private property.

Utilitarianism

- Public good
- Market capitalism
- Pleasure principle
- Relativity

Rights of individuals are largely irrelevant.
Profits are good for all.

Business and ethics

Justice

- Fairness
- Equality
- Equal access to resources

Capitalist societies need to provide for the weak.

Existentialism

- Free will
- Authenticity
- Integrity
- Personal responsibility

Members of corporations should blow the whistle if they see immoral behaviour.

Second, identify the key ideas that are embraced by the subject. Add them to the map in the form of spokes that radiate out from the main subject.

Third, identify the concepts that connect to the key ideas. You can diagram them as branches or networks that grow out of the ideas. If a concept connects to more than one key idea, use different colours or dotted lines to show the relationships. Don't avoid complexity. Multiple connections usually point to interesting issues.

Once the connections are in place, reorganize everything in columns. In many cases, you'll discover that these columns roughly mirror the natural organization of your research and provide an outline for your essay.

Above is an example of a completed mind map. The main subject, business and ethics, sits in the middle. The four key ideas – rights, utilitarianism, existentialism, and justice – top the various columns. The concepts, such as human dignity, public good, free will, and fairness, are listed below them.

Mind mapping is a useful technique. Next time you're stuck, whether at school or at work, try this approach!

CHAPTER 7
Practical Problem Solving for School, Work, and Life

Look and you will find it – what is unsought will go undetected.

— **Sophocles**

The critical skills that you learn at university will make you a more intelligent and valuable employee. In a perfect world, critical and applied skills would be synonymous. Unfortunately, there is often a gap between theoretical learning and practical application that gets in the way of effective problem solving on the job. Many employers complain that new staff have state-of-the-art knowledge but can't apply it to real world situations.

By personal inclination and professional occupation, many university instructors have a preference for abstract and theoretical material. This does not mean that their research and teaching lack significance in the real world. Regardless, your professors are not responsible for showing you how to get, keep, and succeed in a job. You need to take the initiative for yourself.

In this chapter, our focus shifts to the applied skills that allow you to succeed in a competitive marketplace. They're useful to anyone, including your professors! And when combined with the writing, reading, listening, and critical skills discussed in the previous chapters, they are all the more effective.

Why applied problem solving is so important

Your employers are looking for evidence of real world problem-solving skills. Although the capacity to solve problems may be an innate human trait, the ability to solve complex problems separates an extraordinary person from an ordinary one. People who can solve problems stand apart from the rest, are admired by others, and are sought out by employers.

We sometimes see problem solving as the mysterious mark of a superior intellect or genius. But as the proverb suggests, genius is 10 percent inspiration and 90 percent perspiration. Solving a complex problem is hard work. You must take the time to define it, identify its root causes, explore the possible solutions, and choose the best one. Even then, the job is not finished, because you need to apply the solution and evaluate how well it works.

You'd be amazed at how many people in positions of authority or importance take shortcuts or rely on hunches when it comes to problem solving, often with predictable results. To be sure, intuition will occasionally get you through, and you should never ignore it. But if you rely on intuition, guesswork, or – the worst enemy of all – false assumptions, your chances of success are poor.

What happens when you don't solve problems properly? First, you waste valuable time and resources by doing things in a less efficient way. Second, you usually end up applying a band-aid solution rather than actually fixing the problem. Third, many of your efforts will become habits and self-reinforcing assumptions about how to proceed, taking you further and further away from the optimal solution.

In today's highly competitive world, there is little room for such a waste of energy. Those who attempt to solve problems by using guesswork, habit, or false assumptions will be surpassed by those who can identify and remedy them effectively. This is why many corporations now stress problem solving as a necessary characteristic for new employees. But you don't need to limit problem solving to business. It's a life skill. We all face problems in our lives. If we fail to identify and act on the root of our problems, we are doomed to failure in terms of self-discovery, healthy relationships, and reaching our goals.

By learning to problem solve intelligently, you improve your chances of success in your profession and in your life. It's one of the best investments that you can make. And in comparison with other investments, it's relatively simple and straightforward. Acquiring a university education or professional accreditation takes years, but you can begin implementing your improved problem-solving skills as soon as you finish reading this chapter.

Problem solving as a process

The single biggest obstacle to successful problem solving is the tendency to rush to a solution. Problems make people uncomfortable, and the natural inclination is to come up with a solution almost immediately as the best way of restoring their comfort zone. Thereafter, they to cling to their solution and will even defend it aggressively against better alternatives.

Consider, for example, the nature of most class debates in high school. The teacher poses a question (questions are really problems in disguise), students choose their positions, and the dialogue begins. Stances quickly harden, and the debaters themselves become dogmatic. This kind of debate is usually won by the most forceful personalities or the most articulate. Only rarely, and only in the hands of good teachers, do debates prompt individuals to seriously reconsider their initial assumptions. Moreover, however much the participants may enjoy them, they rarely provide new or deeper insights into the problem.

Problem solving at higher levels may feel unnatural at first. It means going slow and being careful. It requires suspending the rush to judgment that might obscure the complexities of the problem and prevent possible solutions. It means being at least as concerned about the route as the destination. It means mapping out that route with care. And it provides results!

Consider a criticism that women sometimes direct at the men in their lives – that they'd rather swallow tacks than ask for directions. This scenario is a fairly simple example of the lack of effective problem-solving skills, but its consequences aren't very serious. People may get lost, waste their time, and become annoyed with each other, but someone will eventually ask for directions and they'll finally reach their destination. Hopefully, their relationship won't suffer too much.

In life and work, the lack of effective problem-solving skills can be much more serious. If a husband and wife have problems with communication, for example, they may assume things about each other that will ultimately destroy the marriage. If a manager assumes that his employees are unproductive because they are lazy, when the problem is actually one of inadequate tools or motivation, he can bring down morale and even ruin the business. If a financial company invests its clients' funds in real estate assuming that the booming housing market will continue, it could destroy the retirement plans of hundreds of families when house sales decline. These and similar scenarios occur every day.

Because inadequate problem solving can produce such destructive results, the best strategy is to opt for a *model* that avoids the typical pitfalls. In this model, we advocate *expanding* the problem first and *contracting* it later.

If we were to begin by limiting the problem or trying to solve it quickly, we would do ourselves a disservice. In the first place, we'd be artificially narrowing the scope of investigation, obscuring the possible causes of the problem, and limiting our ability to gain insights. Only after we've explored the problem in some detail, and deferred judgment on the solution, should we begin to focus more tightly on the root causes.

In the initial stages, expand the problem – identify it and its potential causes from as many angles as possible. This may involve doing a little research. If others have already studied the problem, why not benefit from their work? Exploring the theoretical literature is worth doing. As we pointed out in earlier chapters, concepts and theories are the most sophisticated problem-solving tools. Are there any that apply directly to your problem? Can any theoretical frameworks be adapted to explore it more deeply?

An effective way of researching or brainstorming a problem is as part of a group. This gets as many opinions on the table as possible. The best problem solvers don't chain themselves to their desk and work in isolation – they look for *input*. Lots of input. Ideally, the members of your team will have differing academic or life backgrounds and will bring various theoretical perspectives and personal orientations to bear on the problem. If you are obliged to work on your own, your best strategy is to be as open as possible to the problem and its potential causes, and to explore as many viewpoints as you can.

A major obstacle to effective problem solving, and to decision making in general, is the failure to involve those whose input is most valuable. This mistake is all too common among corporate executives who neglect to consult with co-workers, such as area managers and front-line staff, who have the most detailed knowledge related to the problem. In some instances, the least powerful employees, such as those who deal with customer complaints on a daily basis, can make the best suggestions. No one would ever confuse a modern corporation with a democracy, but the manager who fails to solicit input from all relevant employees is probably not very good at solving problems.

In the early stages of problem solving, function is much more important than form. In other words, don't get hung up on the rules; just go ahead and do the job. Encourage brainstorming and alternative positions rather than focusing on too many rules. For example, you can use diagramming – such as the mind map discussed in the previous chapter – but this is just a tool to help you visualize the problem. Once you have amassed sufficient data, however, processing them in a rigorous way becomes much more important. At this point, you'll want to be more strategic as you move toward solving your problem. You will be *contracting* the information in ways that are increasingly precise.

Many people think that their work is done once they arrive at a solution. Not so. They need to decide how to apply the solution and who will do it. And they're not finished yet. Problem solving is a continual and open-ended activity. In many instances, you won't know whether a problem is fixed until you have hard evidence of success. Also, real life is messy. You may have addressed the initial problem, but new ones can arise as a result. Success in one area can lead to hitches in another. Thus, you need to determine both the negative and the positive outcomes of applying a solution. And finally, the world is constantly changing, which means that you'll need to reassess both the nature of the problem and its solution, sometimes more than once.

Solving problems effectively is difficult, but at the same time doing so is not mysterious. Following the seven steps outlined below will allow you to productively resolve just about any problem.

Step one: defining the problem

Defining a problem should be a fairly simple exercise, right? Wrong! You'd be surprised by the many different ways in which a single problem can be described. Thus, it must be clearly defined and agreed upon by those who are concerned with its solution. This entails

▸ stating it in an objective and factual manner
▸ excluding potentially misleading ambiguities
▸ defining it in such a way that it is solvable.

Consider the following problem statement:

> First-year students are unprepared for university because they weren't taught to read or write adequately in high school.

University instructors often generate similar statements. Nonetheless, this one is unhelpful because it makes implicit assumptions that could get in the way of finding a solution. The assumptions are as follows:

▸ The problem originates in high school. This claim already implies a *cause*, thereby excluding other possible causes.
▸ Students need to be taught better in high school. This assumption implies a *solution* – that high school education needs to change.

What if high school weren't the only, or main, cause of the problem? Can you think of other possible causes? As it stands, doesn't the statement seem to absolve your professors of the responsibility for helping you to develop your reading and writing skills?

The statement is also unhelpful because its unspoken solution isn't useful to those who have identified the problem. It offers professors no guidance on helping their students to improve their skills. If a problem statement is to be useful, it needs to be relevant.

You could also beef up the statement by including a goal. This helps everyone to concentrate on outcomes. It does have a few potential drawbacks, however: the goal could be unrealistic, or unnecessarily restrictive, or it could obscure other possible options.

Here's how you might rewrite the problem statement to include desirable goals:

> Forty percent of first-year university students fail or drop at least one course. Within two years, this university will reduce this to 30 percent.

Note that we've assigned ourselves a deadline for achieving our goal. Again, this focuses everyone on the seriousness of the problem and encourages solving it within a realistic time frame. Of course, a rigid timetable might not be workable with every aspect of a problem. In this case, you can differentiate between long-term goals, whose deadlines could be more fluid, and the measurable short-term steps that lead to them.

Step two: discovering causes

We use the word "discovering" deliberately here. Finding the causes of a problem resembles an exploration more than an exercise in logic. At this point, logic is not the best tool because it can prevent you from keeping your options open. Logic wants you to tighten and restrict your causes, whereas your goal is to be as inclusive as possible.

First, list all the potential causes of the problem, not eliminating anything, no matter how silly it might seem. To diagram this brainstorming exercise, you can use the mind map described in the last chapter. Simply write down as many ideas as you can. Then determine which ones relate to each other and draw connecting lines between them.

Next, begin to organize the ideas a bit more systematically. Here, you could use a fishbone diagram to help you organize major

FISHBONE DIAGRAM

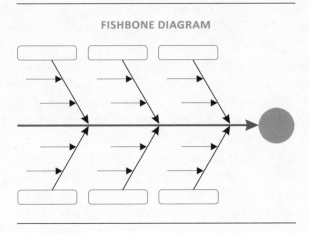

and minor causes. A fishbone diagram resembles the skeleton of a fish. Along the spine, you can add as many ribs as you need. These list your major causes. Lesser bones – the minor causes – dangle from them. It is a good idea to divide the rib bones into categories to make them easier to organize.

For example, in the case of first-year university students, a fishbone model might look like this. The head (round) part is the outcome (many first-year students failing or dropping out). The large bones (the rectangular boxes) are the major or primary causes of this, while the lesser bones show less important or contributing causes. The latter might include

▶ under-developed critical skills
▶ differing learning styles from those acquired in high school
▶ poor time-management and organizational skills
▶ the need to work full- or part-time while at school.

Your work is not yet finished! While still in this step, you need to move toward identifying the *primary causes*. This involves judgment. Whereas we advised you against prematurely rushing to judgment, you should now have collected sufficient information to assess the alternatives.

How you go about doing this will have enormous consequences for everything that comes next. For example, you might decide that the main cause of students' difficulties is their need to work part- or full-time to finance their education. Here, applying a Marxist theoretical framework might be enlightening, as it suggests that unequal access to economic resources is the major problem or source of conflict in capitalist society. Unless the fundamental economic problem is dealt with, most solutions will be no more than temporary or band-aid fixes. However, if you conclude that first-year students experience difficulty at school because the university fails to accommodate their learning styles, none of this will apply, and you will move in a very different direction.

Some primary causes can be related to subordinate causes. For example, students whose paid employment interferes with their studies could benefit from better time management skills. But that kettle of fishbones (if you'll pardon the pun) is very different from saying that students fail primarily because they don't manage their time. Given that many students now work full-time while attending university, they presumably have adequate time management skills. Adopting a Marxist theoretical perspective might allow you to recognize the inherent *bias* in approaches that blame victims for their own victimization.

How do you identify primary and subordinate causes? To find the primary, or *root*, causes, you must subject each of your causes to a battery of "why" questions. In other words, keep asking why until you get as close to the bottom of the matter as possible. Let's try this with the problem of failure among beginning university students.

Why do many first-year students fail or drop out? Answer: because they lack the necessary critical skills to succeed at school. Why do they lack these skills? Answer: because their university courses don't really provide them, and because they themselves don't acquire them on their own.

Why do they not develop their skills? They don't manage their time effectively, either to make use of the available resources or in working on their own. Why do they fail to manage their time? There could be more than one cause for this. As we suggest in this book, many students don't realize that the skills required for success at school will apply equally well in a professional job. Another cause might be that they work such long hours that they barely have enough time for their studies, let alone developing their critical skills.

Why do they spend so much time working? Is it because they come from lower-income families and must therefore finance their own education? Or is it because summer and part-time jobs pay so poorly that they must work long hours before they manage to save money? Or is it because they wish to buy certain things: cars, clothes, smartphones? Or is it because the cost of tuition is high?

Of course, you don't need to agree with any or all of these possible reasons. Our sole purpose here is to show you how to ask why questions to discover the root of the problem. If students must work long hours to pay their tuition, they won't have much time for academic development. Even if resources were made available to them in the form of writing workshops, critical skills seminars, and personal counselling, they might not have the time or energy to use them. Bursaries, on-line instruction, being permitted to study part-time, and the like may be more important to their success than well-intentioned measures that don't go to the source of the problem.

RELATIONSHIP BETWEEN THEORIES AND APPLIED PROBLEM SOLVING

Theories are systematic vehicles for asking why and getting to the root of problems. They help to avoid analytical dead ends and encourage you to identify any assumptions that you might be making.

Problem solving without using theories is a lot like trying to reinvent the wheel. It's a trial-and-error process that achieves mixed results. That's why it's so important to keep abreast of the theoretical literature in your chosen field.

If you remember that theories are the most sophisticated and best-tested problem-solving tools, you will save yourself a lot of unnecessary work.

Step three: establishing solutions

Once you've identified the problem and its primary causes, you will have wasted your time if you don't suggest an appropriate solution. Ideal solutions don't usually exist on their own. They are governed by habits, customs, procedures, and organizational rules, not to mention such obvious limitations as time and money.

When you were defining the problem and looking for causes, you had relatively few constraints apart from common sense. Once you start identifying solutions in any organization or relationship, you'll find yourself beset by naysayers. This is one reason why it's important to re-apply the process that you used when you looked for causes. In other words, you want to *expand* your horizons before *compressing or contracting* them. Sometimes a route that seems impossible turns out to be entirely achievable but only if you seriously explore it as a possibility. Just because something seems foreign or unusual doesn't mean that it might not be a viable solution.

So begin by generating a *longer* rather than a shorter list of options. Use the brainstorming technique to create the list and include *everything* on the first go-around. Here are some tips for brainstorming solutions:

▸ Don't prejudge anything. Many scientists initially thought that global warming was nonsense.
▸ Encourage thinking outside the box.
▸ Be prepared to go beyond your personal opinions, habits, and experience.
▸ Fully explore each solution, even if it seems silly.

Eventually, you will need to shorten your list. But before you delete a solution, check whether it might work well in tandem with another. Sometimes solutions that function poorly in isolation can be powerful team players.

Step four: making a choice

Choosing the best solution means narrowing down the possibilities. In doing this, you must take a rigorous approach, given the practical realities that you and your organization face. The best way of making a choice is to establish the *criteria* for choosing, determine their importance, and establish something like a points system to measure the various solutions.

Large public- and private-sector organizations apply a similar approach all the time, including when they hire staff. Their human resources departments generate a list of criteria for interviewing potential employees. This counters the natural human impulse to focus on a candidate's personality and performance during an interview rather than on his or her real strengths. When every candidate is asked questions that are based specifically on the hiring criteria, a great deal of bias and personal favouritism is eliminated.

Similarly, if you list five or more criteria for evaluating the solutions, you stand a much better chance of choosing the best one. Such criteria can be fairly straightforward:

▸ cost
▸ ease of implementation
▸ chances of success
▸ extent to which the problem is eliminated
▸ potential buy-in of members of the organization.

All these criteria need to be weighed. You might think that eliminating the problem is the most important, but maybe not. If doing so would alienate many members of your organization or its clients, solving the problem probably won't top your list. Conversely, if buy-in isn't a crucial consideration, it will be accorded a lesser weight.

Here is a set of criteria that a university might apply in attempting to reduce the number of first-year students performing poorly in their studies. In this case, the various criteria have been weighted, and their importance is indicated by a percent score:

▸ cost (25 percent)
▸ ease of implementation (35 percent)
▸ chances of success (15 percent)
▸ elimination of problem (25 percent).

For most market-driven businesses, the chances of success and the elimination of the problem would score higher. In a public institution such as a university, however, other factors might be more important.

The crucial element is to have criteria, to assess them, and to rank their importance. If this step is omitted, the adopted solution might not work best for the organization. Dating services do this kind of ranking all the time as they address a particular type of problem: matching people. To do this, they ask clients to rank criteria for the perfect partner. One person might use the following:

▷ attractiveness (25 percent)
▷ intelligence (20 percent)
▷ sense of humour (15 percent)
▷ appreciation of nature (15 percent)
▷ compatibility (20 percent)
▷ income (5 percent).

These percentages will differ from client to client. How would you rank your ideal partner? Do you think that establishing relevant criteria beforehand would help you make a better choice and avoid incompatibility problems later on?

As discussed in Chapter 9, employers use the same kind of ranking when they interview candidates for a job. For example, an employer might use this scheme for a particular position:

▷ communication skills (30 percent)
▷ problem solving (10 percent)
▷ teamwork (35 percent)
▷ flexibility (25 percent).

Step five: implementation

Moving from strategic thinking to purposeful action involves three steps that are very often overlooked, even in large corporations where ineffective action could be disastrous. To apply your solution, you need to develop an *action plan*, or timetable for implementation. Its three steps consist of

1 breaking the solution into specific stages
2 choosing a deadline for each stage
3 deciding who will ensure their completion.

Until an action plan is fully implemented, it's more of a blueprint than anything else. It's not a legal document in which certain conditions or obligations absolutely must be met. For this reason, anyone who develops an action plan might also want to create a parallel *contingency plan.* Its purpose is to anticipate possible problems with implementation and to suggest options for dealing with them.

You can develop a contingency plan by identifying whatever might go wrong in each major step of the action plan. It won't be as specific, but it should be more than an afterthought. In addition, those who are responsible for applying the action plan should be familiar with it for the following reasons:

▷ They will know exactly what to do if the plan is delayed, or if new circumstances make changes necessary.
▷ They will be able to tweak the plan to smooth the transition to the contingency plan.
▷ Knowing that options exist will increase the confidence with which they handle unexpected developments.
▷ Overall, they will take more responsibility.

Authoritarian, or *top-down,* managers who are too controlling and who believe too strongly in their own power sometimes make the mistake of concealing the contingency plan from those who are responsible for implementation. They assume that employees will use the contingency plan as an excuse to depart from the preferred action plan. Most progressive theories of management frown on such a negative approach, particularly with respect to professionals, whose stake in an organization's success often equals that of their superiors.

Step six: benchmarking and evaluating

How do you know if your action and contingency plans are on target? At the end of the day, how will you know that you're succeeding in eliminating the problem? Many organizations develop and implement elaborate plans but shy away from evaluating their progress. Here's how to avoid making this mistake:

1 Establish *benchmarks* to assess your progress.
2 Gather *data* that reveal whether your solution is succeeding or failing.
3 Choose the *criteria* that will evaluate the overall outcome.

Step seven: remaining vigilant

Once the action plan succeeds and the goal is attained, you need to do one last thing – establish guidelines to ensure that the problem will *not recur*. The problem with problems is that many are like bad habits: you may get rid of them, but they tend to resurface the minute you relax. Given that solving a problem requires so much hard work, ensuring that it doesn't come back is certainly worth the effort.

For example, let's say you're in a flawed relationship with a member of the opposite, or same, sex. After identifying the root problem(s), you can try to address it by applying a joint solution. Or you can extricate yourself from the situation and find someone new. But if you don't take care not to reproduce the bad relationship, the problem will almost certainly reappear.

Problem solving as a life skill

Our focus in this chapter has been on applied problem solving for organizations. But problem solving isn't unique to professional employees. It's useful in every aspect of life and is essential for identifying and reaching life goals. Building good relationships and dissolving potential or real clashes with others are of crucial importance. Getting to the root of personal conflicts is the first step toward creating a mutually agreeable solution.

It's a good idea to strengthen problem-solving skills before you graduate, if only because prospective employers will be looking for evidence that you possess these important skills. You will not achieve perfect mastery, but you'll certainly have some life experiences that reveal your problem-solving skills and professional potential. During a job interview, candidates are commonly asked to "describe a problem that you had at work, school, or with other people and tell us how you dealt with it." If you can show prospective employers that you have used some of the seven steps above in dealing with complexities, you will be a much more attractive candidate.

CHAPTER 8
Creative Problem Solving for Life and Work

> Trust that still, small voice that says, "This might work and I'll try it."
>
> — Diane Mariechild

As any self-respecting artist will tell you, creativity is its own very best reward. It enchants life and makes it worth living. But creative thinking is also a highly prized attribute, especially in our complex world. The pace of life and its preoccupation with technology reinforce *experiential* and *reactive* ways of reasoning that seduce us "into confusing action for thought and passive entertainment for creative participation."[8] In our highly stimulated society, creative thinking is on the decline. Those who demonstrate it are in increasingly short supply.

Some people think that creativity is genetic. If you're not born with it, you don't have it. You often hear people say, "I'm not very creative," as if their lack of creativity were cast in stone. The reality is that everyone possesses creativity. Have you ever noticed how creative children are when they play? Imagination makes all things possible for them. They have a remarkable ability to forge magical alliances between themselves and their environment. Recapturing that childlike approach can contribute to your happiness and success in life.

Those who suggest that creativity can't be taught have a point. Being creative is more about *freeing* something that may have become *blocked* by many years of learning other valuable types of knowledge. Enhancing your creativity means letting go of overly rigid habits.

The good news is that you can learn how to do this by applying certain techniques. And ironically, you can acquire these techniques in a logical and systematic way.

Relation to problem solving

Most problem solving relies on logic and experience. It works with hard facts, and it deploys conceptual tools to organize information. Creativity involves a different set of mental muscles. A fluid and flexible form of *reflective reasoning*, it is characterized by "top-down processing." The human brain creates its own reality rather than simply reacting to it. But the mind doesn't exist in isolation, and creativity isn't developed in a vacuum.

Many problems can be solved by using the steps outlined in the last chapter. But some examples won't fit into an established pattern or routine, and addressing them requires a more creative approach. In their case, it is important to become more spontaneous and uninhibited in your thinking.

Creative thinking is fun. It is inherently playful. That's why children usually have a much greater capacity for creativity than adults. They take the time for mental play and are highly motivated to be creative. We adults ignore this childlike capacity at our peril, because the most difficult and important problems in life, school, and work won't always lend themselves to straightforward or logical answers. By taking an overly rationalistic approach, we restrict our ability to find solutions.

Most of us will develop some facility with rational problem solving. Many university graduates, but certainly not all, possess this skill. What differentiates creative problem solvers from *typical* problem solvers is their ability to confront and solve the problems that stymie most people.

Here's a little test of your creative thinking. Drop a dime into an empty wine bottle and then cork the bottle. Your task is to retrieve the dime without pulling the cork or breaking the bottle. The solution involves thinking outside your regular mental box.

WHAT SCIENTISTS HAVE LEARNED

Science suggests that conventional problem solving occurs primarily in the left side of the brain, whereas the right side handles more divergent or creative approaches to reality. All children are "creativity engines," but their talent for right-brain thinking is slowly repressed and becomes more difficult to access as they grow up. The left side of the brain literally takes over.

Conventional intelligence does not equate with creative intelligence. In fact, when the left brain is damaged, greater creative powers are often unleashed. This occurs because logic and memory lose control over some of the brain's functions. This ability to "let go" is a creative characteristic.

Over-specialized thinking can also hinder creativity. When experts adhere too rigidly to disciplinary models, they tend to lose their capacity for conceptual flexibility. If their approach doesn't work, they usually find themselves at a "mental dead end." That is why using a multi- or interdisciplinary approach is inherently more creative than relying on just one discipline.

Ideally, however, creativity involves a marriage of the left and right sides of the brain. The most useful ideas combine imaginative thinking with theoretical and disciplinary knowledge. For example, Albert Einstein's (1879-1955) theory of relativity, perhaps the most famous creative breakthrough, was grounded in his expert understanding of conventional physics and mathematics.[9]

Did you consider pushing the cork down inside the bottle? Good for you!

The goal of puzzles like this is to reveal how rigidly we structure our minds and to accustom us to thinking *outside the box*.

The rigid structures of the mind

Becoming a creative thinker involves eliminating some major obstacles. Unless these are eradicated, the techniques for more creative thinking won't have a chance to take hold. You can discover some of these barriers for yourself by thinking of the differences between children and adults that allow the former to be more creative. The five major obstacles to becoming more creative are discussed below.

COMPLACENCY

Complacency means being lazy about thinking: you can't be bothered; it's just too much work. This attitude prevents you from applying your curiosity. Just consider how often young children ask "why" and how intensely curious they are. Recapture some of that curiosity! To do that, be prepared to think.

Let yourself be curious. Spare some time for thinking. Think about all kinds of things that seem to have nothing to do with your job, school assignments, or immediate experience. Let your mind wander and explore again.

FEAR

Fear is the creative mind killer. The dread of making a mistake or looking foolish shuts down imaginative thought. Small children have no such anxiety and go boldly where adults fear to tread. Creative people attribute their creativity to the fact that they are not afraid to look stupid.

To be a creative thinker, you need to take risks. You need to be courageous. Creative people explore lots of options, most of which will be unsatisfactory. The fact that they are willing to look at problems in unique ways means that many of their analyses and proposed solutions will seem strange to others. But it also means that their solutions to problems will be original, unique, and successful.

CONSISTENCY/CONSTANCY

Oscar Wilde (1854-1900) once remarked that "consistency is the last refuge of the unimaginative." What he meant was that people who think in overly linear or rigid terms are not capable of creativity. To be a creative problem solver, you must apply different kinds of thinking. You need to think laterally – looking for associations, similarities, linkages – as well as vertically or logically. You need to picture the problem symbolically and visually, not simply in terms of verbal reasoning.

To arrive at solutions, you must step outside the box. This is more important than getting hooked on finding the right answer.

STEREOTYPING

To stereotype is to group things together on the basis of their perceived similarities. We use it every day as we organize our lives, so it isn't necessarily a bad thing. But it can be an obstacle to creativity whenever it blurs subtleties or ignores differences. The worst kind of stereotyping is black-and-white thinking – dividing people and data into highly simplistic and restrictive categories such as right and wrong, good and evil, us and them, familiar and unfamiliar.

University education tries to go beyond the stereotyping of everyday life by asking students to look for subtleties, ambiguities, and differences. Then it gets them to recombine information into completely new, deeper, and more complex and meaningful categories.

But a university education sometimes achieves the opposite. Dogmatic teaching methods, narrow-minded scholarly disciplines, and overly rigid theories can prevent new ideas from percolating to the mind's surface.

COMPRESSING/REDUCING

We have a natural tendency to reduce a problem into something manageable. In fact, this occurs so quickly that we don't have a chance to see the problem differently or to explore different options. That's because we are too eager to rid ourselves of the problem.

Being creative involves reversing this habit. You need to expand the problem, looking at it in various ways and from different angles. Eventually, of course, you'll want to solve it, but your solutions will be more interesting if you expand it first. You can't be creative if you narrow the problem too quickly; you can't illuminate it unless you look at it from a variety of positions; you can't incubate creative thinking unless you play with many approaches.

One of the best ways to expand a problem is to examine it through the conceptual lens of a theory (see the previous chapters). Many theories are revolutionary, not necessarily in terms of

A COMMENT ON BUSINESS EDUCATION

In our opinion, contemporary business education suffers enormously due to its habit of compressing and reducing problems. It relies unduly on the case study method and bottom-line thinking. Case studies are in-depth reports on a specific situation or event in order to understand what happened and why. However, they have a tendency to fossilize information and examples within overly simplistic formulas. Right from the start, the preferred solution is typically embedded in the problem. Consequently, once business students grasp this approach, they usually apply it mechanically and routinely, without further thought.

The preoccupation with the bottom line (profit) is extremely short-sighted, and it underscores many dilemmas faced by individuals, business corporations, and governments. Too much focus on the bottom line undermines creative possibilities that could contribute to the long-term viability of organizations, not to mention more meaningful working environments.

Conventional problem solving obviously has its proper time and place. But if business schools really want their students to become creative problem solvers – as they often claim – they need to embed creative thinking more firmly in their curricula.

advocating radical change, but in *transforming* how we see the world. Being creative involves thinking at the deeper levels that characterize theoretical understanding. At the same time, be careful not to lose the element of play if you want to apply theories creatively.

Creative problem-solving techniques

Now that you have a better understanding of some of the obstacles, we can begin to discuss techniques for increasing creativity. Remember, *everyone* has the capacity for creative thought. Originality is much more widely dispersed than most people imagine. The trick is tapping into it. Here's how:

1 The first and most difficult task (but ultimately the most fun) is to recover our curiosity and wonderment about the world and people. This is difficult to do in our day-to-day activities, where custom and habit have made us rigid. That's why we need to re-engineer the process by reading, thinking, and exploring subjects that are less familiar to us. Reading, watching television programs, seeing movies, or talking to people on topics that interest us, but are not necessarily *useful*, is one of the best ways to do this.

   When we expand our minds on less familiar territory, we give ourselves fresh information to explore in a more playful manner. What is surprising, even magical, is the way that this new information invariably affects the other areas of our lives by allowing us to make novel connections and to see new possibilities. Again, don't overlook the theoretical frameworks that you learn at university as potentially fresh ways of seeing and exploring the world.

   Sometimes we don't even need external sources of stimulation to revitalize us. If we simply set aside time to think, meditate, or just *be*, our minds may empty momentarily, leaving some room for new ideas to come in. If our minds keep chattering in old accustomed ways, it's hard for anything new and exciting to appear.

   It goes without saying that this process requires free time. Having a balanced lifestyle is critical to creativity. The saying "all work and no play makes Jill a dull girl and Jack a dull boy" is entirely appropriate when it comes to freeing creativity.

2 Our second suggested technique aims at *shaking up* your customary mental approaches and habits. Because these are so ingrained, you really need to practise a mental transformation. You can achieve this by teaching yourself to *make the familiar strange*, an approach that can enable you to see things in brand new ways. Simply use your imagination, or if you can afford it, travel to a new environment.

   An anthropologist once described the ritual behaviour of a strange tribe whose male members daily went into a small but brightly lit room. In that locked cubicle, they took a sharp blade and scraped a layer of skin from their faces. Sometimes they accidentally cut themselves, and the blood had to be soaked up with cloth. Despite all the mess and pain, however, they routinely went through this barbaric procedure every day.

What on earth do you think the anthropologist was describing? Would you believe it was the act of shaving in a bathroom? Notice how this commonplace behaviour becomes a strange ritual when made unfamiliar. Now consider the many ways that you can enrich your understanding of everyday experiences by making them less familiar. Most students study for at least four years before they are allowed to work at a professional job. How strange is that? Many people work nine-to-five, live only for the weekend, and detest their jobs. Isn't that a weird way to live? A medieval peasant or tribal warrior would certainly think so.

And what about shopping for clothes and other goods? Our ancestors might see that as peculiar, obsessive, and psychologically disturbing. In fact, being a *consumer* might not be a very sensible way to live at all! Could someone from the past make sense of the expression "Shop till you drop"?

3 Defer judgment. We tend to define both a problem and its solution far too quickly. This is a recipe for uncritical and uncreative behaviour. To appreciate great art or literature, we must give it some time and hold back on judging. We need to explore the subject matter or problem in greater depth. We have to let it *speak to us*.

Many first-year university students have real trouble with this. They swiftly decide whether they like or dislike something and have a tendency to dismiss difficult literature or creative ideas as boring or unintelligible (or both). They need to learn to look on a new subject, text, or scholarly discipline as a challenge, not a consumer choice.

You'll never learn to think creatively unless you give problems and topics the benefit of the doubt. You can't be a creative problem solver unless you go beneath the surface to explore something in depth.

Creative thinking has a lot in common with critical thinking. Both are the opposite of superficial thinking. They move deeply as well as laterally and are rarely passive. They don't accept information or ideas at face value, but look for less obvious and even hidden meanings. Critical and creative thinking are both highly *reflective* approaches to learning. The main difference between them is that critical thinking is usually guided by logical rules, whereas creative thinking dispenses with these rules and retains an element of play.

4 A related technique involves looking at data or problems from odd or unusual perspectives. That's exactly what Einstein did when he considered the universe. At that time, most scientists believed that the universe functioned like a giant clock. In other words, it behaved like a perfect machine, and all its parts were connected in a linear fashion by cause-and-effect relationships. This clockwork universe was grounded in the unquestioned idea that time and space are constant.

Einstein allowed his mind to make this mechanical universe more fuzzy and problematic. He was able to see space as curved rather than linear. Moreover, he saw that time and space might not be constant, but relative to the perception of the viewer. As he put it, a minute can seem like an hour when you are sitting on a hot stove, but an hour can seem like a minute when you are in the arms of a hot date.

A more down-to-earth example of approaching a problem from an unusual angle involves a parade that was staged every year by a number of community groups. Becoming concerned about liability, the local city hall instructed the parade organizers to buy insurance to cover any damage or accidents that might occur during the event. Since the community groups couldn't afford insurance, the popular parade seemed doomed to extinction.

Instead, they came up with an ingenious solution – to hold a *stationary parade* in a large field. As long as the parade didn't move, no insurance was needed. The community groups creatively redefined the concept of a parade to solve their dilemma. The annual stationary parade became a social and economic success.

5 Yet another tried-and-true technique of creativity is the imaginative use of *symbols*. Artists, singers, actors, and writers are prized in society – some becoming rich and famous – because they are creativity experts. Instead of presenting information logically, they use symbols, metaphors, and analogies. Playing with symbols

allows them to visualize the world in deeper, richer, and more interesting ways.

6 When you're stuck on a problem or can't come up with a creative thought to save your life, try using prepositions to redefine the problem. Prepositions are words such as near, with, under, as, to, among, over, through, about, against, between, for, on, after, across, opposite. You can probably think of a lot more.

Let's say that your problem relates to two major elements – *customers* and *service*. By replacing the word "and" with various prepositions, you can create entirely new and inventive combinations, or equations:

- Customers *near* service might suggest that you need to bring your service operations closer to your customers.
- Customers *with* service implies that your customers will serve you: they bring you valuable information about your product.
- Customers *under* service indicates that service could be an umbrella to protect customers – an interesting brand identification that has possibilities.
- Customers *as* service could mean that customers provide service to each other; a happy customer could be a great indirect salesperson.

By now you are thinking more creatively. Maybe you noticed that we could *reverse* the equation by putting the service first:

▹ Service *before* customers might mean that the service needs of customers should be anticipated before they come in for service.

▹ Service *over* customers suggests placing greater emphasis on service and less on sales. This might diminish the need for sales staff since the service will bring people back.

▹ Service *during* customers implies providing service in a timely manner.

▹ Service *after* customers means ensuring that service continues after the sale and that customers are informed of it.

Creatively reconfiguring the problem

Since the problem itself is the focus of so much creative motivation and energy, one approach to solving it is to manipulate its definition. As we saw above, playing with prepositions is one way of achieving this. But there are other ways of making the problem work for us.

The first and most obvious is to ask whether the problem can be stated differently. Taking this step enables novel solutions to arise. For example, cellphones were originally intended for emergency communication. They were big, clunky, and expensive to produce. When they were redefined as *chat* devices, their potential took off, and now they access the Internet, track friends, navigate city streets, monitor health, take pictures, play games and music, and more. Similarly, though the Apple iPad was not the first computer tablet, it redefined what a tablet could and should do, revealing the enormous potential of the product.

Another way is to problematize the definition. When the community groups redefined their parade, they were problematizing the definition of the problem by questioning whether liability or insurance needed to be involved. By focusing on situations where liability did not exist, they escaped the trap posed by the original formulation of the quandary.

Expanding the problem is also an effective approach. Problems are sometimes defined too narrowly to easily permit creative solutions. You can expand a problem by asking the following questions:

- What other problems are similar to this?
- Is it confined to one situation, or is it more general?
- What else can we say about it?
- What are its *meanings* and *results*?

And finally, reversing the problem is similar to problematizing the problem, but easier. Sometimes referred to as Janusian thinking, after the Roman god Janus who had two faces – one looking to the past, the other to the future (the month of January is named after the god). Janusian thinking may suggest that the problem may not be a problem at all if looked at correctly. It also means highlighting opposites in the problem or its definition.

Maximizing creative solutions

An important key to achieving creativity is having a diverse pool of viewpoints from which to draw solutions. This means getting as much input as possible from other people. It also means that collaboration is a terrific vehicle for producing creative solutions.

When multiple perspectives are aimed directly at a particular problem, the chances of finding a creative solution are much better. That's why organizations, which deal with rapid change and global competition, encourage the formation of collaborative groups or project teams. These groups can be put together, pulled apart, and reconstructed in whatever ways guarantee as much input as possible.

Individuals can create their own groups, such as a study group, which often help students in preparing their assignments. If you are part of a group, here are four suggestions:

▷ To stop the group from becoming too hierarchical, give everyone a chance at its various roles.
▷ Encourage members to challenge solutions or play devil's advocate.
▷ People tend to get lazy if they're not pushed, so put someone in charge of *prodding* others to achieve solutions. (Prodding is not an enviable job and no one likes a nag, so be sure to reassign this task often!)
▷ Guard against *groupthink* – when group members think with one mind and become altogether too predictable, narrow, and comfortable.

The right environment for creative thinking

Although teamwork is a potentially useful engine of creativity for the modern organization, it needs a safe and comfortable environment. In the corporate world, teams are temporary structures.

People may legitimately feel that their collaborative virtues are merely being exploited in the interest of productivity and the bottom line. In such situations, both character and creativity will inevitably suffer. People may go through the motions of being team players, but their creativity will not be empowered.

That's why establishing a more continuous and safe environment is so important for creativity. Some environments are better than others. The ideal examples encourage individuals to relax and distance themselves a little from problems. The most difficult problems are often solved when minds are not merely permitted to wander into unrelated areas but are encouraged to do so. This loosens the hold of mental habits and allows original ideas to surface.

One of the authors of this book had the good fortune several years ago to visit a high-tech software company well known for its creative products. The employees were surprisingly relaxed. Instead of being buried in or under their work, they regularly roamed away from their cubicles to talk to each another. The lunchroom fridge was stocked with almost every soft drink, juice, and mineral water available, all of them free. The main office included a pool table, where employees played pool and chatted *during their working hours*.

A great deal of thought went into the creation of this office. Many of its characteristics were designed explicitly to tear down the barriers to communication and to allow employees to break out of rigid mental routines. The physical space was conducive to creative thinking, very different from closed offices or isolated cubicles.

Obviously, not every workplace will look like this. To the extent that you can, you want to create physical and mental environments that allow you to be creative. It's important to recognize that a relaxed environment is different from one that is too comfortable or that has too many distractions. For this reason, it's a good idea to keep the home and the workspace separate, or at least to confine work to a particular area at home.

It is equally important to allow yourself reflective and recharging time when away from the workplace. Passive entertainment can hog the time needed for more *active* and engaged thinking, so turn off the smartphone, tablet, television, and computer.

Don't isolate yourself from people when you work, unless it's to accomplish a particular task. Being with others is healthy. Discussing your work or something you're reading – during a break, for example – stimulates creativity. And as you become more creative, interesting, and informative, you will attract and be attractive to other creative people, and should welcome interaction with them.

There is an important exception to this general rule. Unfortunately, some people will want to benefit from your positive attributes without giving anything in return. Protecting yourself against them or against toxic or negative people is not mean or selfish. Associating with negative individuals negates creativity. Very few people – they do exist and are wonderful – can sustain their own creativity in a negative environment.

Of course, some positive environments can stifle creativity, and it's a good idea to recognize them and to confine them to their appropriate time and place. For example, you may enjoy going out on the town with your friends. By all means, have a good time. But be aware that these outings may not have much to do with creative thought.

It's useful to be aware that some tensions may arise with friends and family as you grow as a person. That's why very creative people usually associate with others who have the same characteristics. At the end of the day, one of the best ways to become and stay creative is simply to hang with those who are. Just remember, always try to give as much creativity as you get!

Faced with school assignments, work commitments, family obligations, and more, we can lose the capacity for getting more deeply in touch with ourselves and with others. In this situation, we don't burn brightly. We just burn out.

As you pursue your university and professional career, it's imperative to be self-nourishing. There is no better way of caring for yourself than developing your creativity. Unlike many tedious aspects of life, it adds delight and mystery. Moreover, it isn't confined to a particular part of life. You can apply it to everything you do, from cooking and needlework to painting, exercising, and writing.

Some people artificially restrict the creative impulse to their hobbies or leisure activities, simply going through the motions at university or in their jobs. They thereby squander a tremendous opportunity to develop and practise skills that are in short supply. If you can apply creativity at school and at work, you will be a far less bored and more highly valued employee.

Look for opportunities to nurture the imagination. Protect the creative child within. Give yourself time to daydream.

CHAPTER 9

Finding and Getting the Great Job

> Keep on going and the chances are you will stumble on
> something, perhaps when you are least expecting it. I have
> never heard of anyone stumbling on something sitting down.
>
> — Charles Kettering

Students who are about to graduate, or who have recently done so, often have no idea where the great jobs are. Studying aspects of current developments in business and politics can be a help in finding them. If a particular industry is booming, or a certain topic is suddenly in the news, many jobs can suddenly open up, from human resources counselling to computer programming. Some of your professors will also be good guides to employment opportunities. After all, part of their job is to be current in their field of expertise.

Be aware, however, that the employment marketplace changes very quickly. Don't choose a major, program, or profession simply because you expect it to provide lots of jobs.

A far better approach is to follow your interests and keep both eyes open for good linkages to the workplace. As we suggest in the previous chapters, use your university years to determine which type of employment will give you the most satisfaction and fit with your skills and interests. This does not mean that you must know exactly what you want to be, just what you like and are good at.

We've stressed that four skills determine success at both school and work:

▶ communication (reading, writing, speaking, listening)
▶ capacity to learn and solve problems
▶ teamwork, including social skills (ethics, positive attitude, responsibility)
▶ adapting to changing circumstances and transferring knowledge to new situations.

Which of these is your particular strength? To determine where you'll flourish in the professional world, you need to rank yourself on all four.

People who choose a career simply for economic and security reasons often have a very poor understanding of who they are and what they want from life. If their career doesn't pan out, they will remain adrift until they do a lot of soul searching.

It is much easier to get work than to discover a professional fit that is right for you. Too many people are unhappy because they are in positions that don't suit their personality. Too many people are trapped in those positions for financial and security reasons. Don't let this happen to you. Think long and hard about the kind of job that suits your temperament, and use your university experience to guide and help you in this process of self-discovery.

Don't be limited by job labels or the expectations of others. If you take the time to make connections, you'll find that your interests and talents match with the marketplace in many ways. The authors of this book may be professional academics, but they have flexible skills and did not follow a straight path to their current jobs.

One, for example, has been at various times an administrator, a placement director for a prestigious business school, and the president of a company that communicated between governments and universities. The other author worked for nearly a decade as a policy advisor in government, was a consultant in Ottawa, and taught in Asia and Europe. All of these jobs were wonderful, and we wouldn't have missed them for the world.

No one steps into the ideal job immediately after leaving university. Reaching the perfect job takes decades. The journey will be more rewarding if you have a destination in mind, based on your interests and skills.

The importance of networking

Networks are the informal and not easily visible human relationships that govern much of what happens in the workplace. No matter how bureaucratic an organization may seem, important decisions such as hiring and promotion are usually based, in part, on networking. Career experts estimate that over 80 percent of jobs are *never* advertised. When a job needs to be filled, employers and managers invariably turn to their own networks.

This makes sense since employers are interested in quickly finding the right person. After all, they tend to hire a new employee only after a mass of urgent work has piled up! Posting a job advertisement, replying to dozens of e-mails, looking at hundreds of resumes, selecting and interviewing candidates, following up references, and negotiating an employment contract take a lot of time. And there is no guarantee that the right person will be chosen. Thus, employers prefer to hire someone who is already known to them or to someone whom they trust.[10]

The ultimate objective of networking is making your name and resume known to as many people as possible. When they hear of an employment opportunity, they'll let you know. This does not automatically mean that the job is yours, only that you might be considered.

Effective networking, therefore, provides you with many potential points of contact during the course of your career. Your network can be your most important tool when it comes to job hunting or promotion.

The statistics bear this out. As the table below reveals, a survey of thousands of individuals in Canada and the United States discovered that nearly half (46 percent) found a job through person-to-person networking.[11]

Route to employment	Percent
Agency/recruiter	14
Direct approach	7
Internet job board	25
Newspaper/periodical	1
Other	7
Networking	46

Forming a group that cooperates in identifying jobs and employers is a particularly effective and innovative way of networking. It pools information and leads. You yourself may not be the right person for a job, but someone else in your group could be, and vice versa. This strategy works well for students who have recently completed their degrees or are about to graduate. It is important to establish your group before you begin to lose touch with many of your university friends.

The sooner you start networking, the better. Most business schools encourage students to begin networking as soon as they enter university, on the grounds that their classmates will eventually be their contacts. What works for business students will work for you. Social media are especially useful here, making networking easier than ever (we'll come back to social media later in this chapter and in the next one).

It's never too late to begin networking. If you haven't already created a list of contacts, start now. Establishing a network that can help you get a professional position takes at least four months. Networks are fragile, however, and will collapse if not actively nurtured. Building them slowly will add strength and stability.

Professional networks make demands on your time and talents. You need time to meet with people for information interviews (discussed below) and may be asked to help with activities or lend a hand in other ways. Any such professional contribution, however, will increase both your skill set and the size and significance of your network. Be dependable and make a solid effort. The grapevine will soon communicate who is reliable and who is not.

Resumes

Your resume reflects your professionalism. An effective resume implies an impressive personality. An actively worded resume implies a proactive individual – the much-sought-after self-starter. A well-organized resume suggests a logical and efficient person.

More nonsense has been written about resumes than almost any other subject. There is no single model that is most effective, although many people would like to think so. A resume does not need to be confined to just one page. A two-page resume that has been gracefully organized will be much easier to read than a crammed single sheet. You can use a coloured font, just as long as you don't overdo it.

The most important characteristic of a good resume is that it reflects the individual whose name appears at the top. The resume is a way of telling others about you. There's no point in making it describe someone who differs from the real you. What purpose would that serve?

Fibbing or exaggerating on a resume may land you a job, but chances are that your boss and colleagues will soon discover that you aren't what you pretended to be. Chances are that the job won't fit with your talents or interests, either. Being yourself, and accurately portraying yourself, is the best way to ensure a satisfying job, career, and life.

Composing a strong resume and cover letter, however, involves more than being accurate and sincere. It requires some of the skills for writing a strong essay. You need to put yourself in the position of the reader and be clear and concise.

Most resume tips are just common sense, especially when you consider how a potential employer will look at a resume:

- If you are a student, or recent graduate, highlight your education and include lots of details, because your education is basically you.
- Write the name of your educational program *exactly* as it appears on your transcript.
- If you've worked full-time for a while, emphasize your employment experience, but remember that your education is crucial as well.
- Include related volunteer experience. It is as important as any other work experience, and it testifies to the kind of person that you are.
- Use active words that emphasize achievements, such as developed, earned, researched, studied, evaluated, improved, learned, and analyzed, rather than passive words such as duties or responsibilities.
- List only those hobbies or interests that relate directly to the position.
- Don't include references. If an employer is interested in you, you'll be asked to provide them.

▸ Never make spelling or grammatical errors. Resumes that include these end up in the recycle bin.

▸ Always enclose a cover letter, even if not requested, that shows why you are right for the job.

Most employers have zero tolerance for sloppy or poorly formatted resumes. If you don't know how to create your own and don't have time to learn, hire someone to do it for you. If cost is a factor, just remember that doing an imperfect job is a waste of your time and money. Even better, look for samples on the Internet, and from friends and family, to build your own resume. We've got excellent samples in this chapter to help you.

You can exponentially increase your chances of a positive reaction to your resume by providing proof that you possess desirable characteristics, such as strong communication skills, teamwork, problem solving, critical and creative skills, the ability to work independently, and multi-tasking. Creative examples of how to do this are given below.

SAMPLE RESUMES

The three resumes in Appendix 1 at the end of this chapter provide models that you might want to consider. Although we have changed the names, the resumes are real and were successful in getting students part-time, summer, and full-time professional jobs.

The key to the success of these resumes is that considerable effort, time, and thought went into them. From the perspective of a potential employer, they provide the kind of information required to decide whether the individual should be interviewed. Note that each one is different since each person is unique, with different employment goals.

The first resume (page 177) belongs to a student who has changed programs, universities, countries, and employers, and is about to graduate. Yet note how clearly this is presented. Note also how much detail is provided regarding his education, including the GPA. In your own resume, feel free to mention the titles of your essays.

The second resume (page 179) is that of a first-year student. Note the choices she made in building her resume, such as not

USEFUL RESUME WRITING HINTS

Hint 1: Use the table feature in your word-processing software to format your resume. Once it's complete, hide the borders. This will allow you to design an interesting resume, which can be easily edited.

Hint 2: Use your university e-mail address. Anyone can get a Gmail account, but not everyone is a university student. You can set up your university e-mail to automatically forward all messages to another account. Oh, and by the way, silly names like megadeath @gmail.com send a totally wrong message to prospective employers.

Hint 3: Always emphasize the position that you held, rather than your employer or place or work. Future employers will be interested in what you did, rather than where you worked. The same applies to your education. Potential employers are less interested in the university you attended than in your specific program of studies and your performance.

referring to her high school experience. The final resume (page 181) illustrates how a student with a limited work history, who has just begun her university studies, has presented her employment to date.

The cover letter

When it comes to getting a professional position, resumes are necessary but nowhere near as important as cover letters. If you aren't asked to submit a cover letter as part of your application, the job will not be a professional one.

The resume speaks to your skills, achievements, and character. The cover letter explains why you are the right choice for this particular position. If you think of it as a marriage proposal, you won't be far off the mark. Employers are looking for a good match between their needs and your potential contribution.

Experienced recruiters and knowledgeable employers are much more interested in your cover letter than in your resume. They'll be hoping to find clues to your personality and to discover why you chose to apply to their company or organization. They'll be flattered if they discover that you are knowledgeable about their reputation and achievements. They'll be annoyed if they suspect that you are randomly applying for positions. Most of all, they will expect you to have done your homework.

Do your research on the company or organization to which you are applying. Before you begin to write your cover letter, you should know as much as possible about the recipients. What philosophy does their organization embrace? Does it have a mission statement? What problems is it currently facing? What problems might it face in the future (such as competitors or changes in demographic trends)? Your cover letter will be much more effective if it shows an appreciation for the organization's achievements, culture, and challenges.

Most of this basic information is posted on the Internet and can be found in sources such as annual reports. However, as a university student who is well versed in research and critical thinking, you can add value to the information that you collect. This will truly set you apart. Perhaps something that you learned from your university essays applies to the company or position. Try to mention it in the cover letter.

If the position has been advertised, respond directly to the wording and tone of the ad. Always try to show that you can supply the required characteristics. Go through them systematically as you address them. Never use a one-size-fits-all letter. Instead, tailor it to the position. If this seems like a lot of work, just consider that the chances of getting short-listed with a form letter are virtually non-existent. Now that's time wasted!

Consider the tone and language of the advertisement. Does it convey dynamism? Is it precise, conservative, detailed, formal, informal? The tone and language are often key indications of what the organization is looking for. Your cover letter will be more effective if it conveys the same characteristics.

Tell potential employers what you can do for them. Students' cover letters typically dwell on the things that an organization can provide and tend to be sketchy regarding how they themselves will contribute to the company. Corporate recruiters routinely weed out those kinds of submissions; they're looking for candidates who are self-starters and proactive problem solvers with up-to-date knowledge acquired from their university courses.

Aim to reveal how you can do the job. The letter should be "forward-looking," as a potential employer is much more interested in what you will accomplish once hired than in what you have done so far.

Take great care with the construction of your letter. The number of resumes that are thrown out because they are accompanied by clumsy and ungrammatical letters would astonish you. Making more than one spelling mistake in a cover letter or resume typically means that it goes straight into the trash bin!

Don't try to be someone that you are not. Apply to companies that are looking for people who have your characteristics. Even if you successfully use the techniques mentioned above to land a job, you won't be happy unless the fit is genuine.

COVER LETTER FORMAT

Most cover letters share the same basic format (as do all documents, be they essays or poems). A common example is on page 182. However, do not feel bound to follow it slavishly: instead, adapt it to fit your particular circumstances. The purpose of the cover letter is to reveal something about you that does not appear in your resume and that will help the employer make a decision.

Try to get the name of the manager who is hiring and use it – "Dear Ms. Park." Remember that this person, not someone in the human resources department, will ultimately decide who is to be hired. You may need to submit your application to the human resources department, but having discovered who is hiring (your future boss) gives your cover letter a special quality. It shows that you are serious.

Start with an introductory paragraph in which you state your interest in the position and try to capture your reader's attention. The language here needs to convey genuine interest without being unprofessional. The hook for the reader is often company-specific knowledge or a compliment (genuine, not flattery). A typical opening might be:

> I recently learned of a six-month contractual position as a junior marketing assistant, with a focus on social media, at TRK Enterprises.

Use the next paragraph to state your strengths and to reveal the added value that you can bring to the organization. A recent graduate might write:

> While earning my BA in English and History at MY University, I studied the use and implications of social media in two fourth-year courses. I have four years of experience working part-time as a salesperson in a company of the same size as TRK Enterprises. My managers rated my work as "excellent, with particular attention to detail."

In the next paragraph, give a more detailed summary of your relevant education and experience. For example, you might identify the specific courses that you took and any special attributes that might help sell you to a potential employer:

> During my BA, my English courses focused on how authors use the printed word to communicate complex feelings and emotions. In my third-year history courses, I studied how Canadian demographic trends of the past fifty years have shaped, and continue to shape, social and economic developments. I have used some of what I learned at university, as well as my knowledge of social media, to create my own website: myownsite.web.

If necessary, you can add a short paragraph to address any problems that an employer is likely to spot. For example, you need to be proactive about gaps in your career:

> Between the third and fourth years of my BA, I took fourteen months to travel and work in East Asia with my sister. This wonderful learning opportunity introduced me to many different

> cultures and attitudes. Although the experience was challenging at times, especially when I worked for four months in a high-end Beijing restaurant, it taught me a great deal about overcoming barriers and interacting with a variety of people.

If possible, add a paragraph to address any problems that the organization is facing. This is a good way to introduce new knowledge or techniques that you learned at university or elsewhere:

> I recently read in the book *The Zen of Social Media Marketing: An Easier Way to Build Credibility* that social media are highly effective in attracting potential consumers, but less so in increasing sales. I am particularly interested in working hard with the experienced marketing staff at TRK Enterprises to help convert potential consumers into long-term clients.

Add one or two sentences that explain how you intend to follow up. You need to demonstrate that you are proactive and won't simply wait passively for a call from the employer:

> I look forward to an opportunity to discuss the position and my contributions in greater detail through a personal interview. I will e-mail or call next Tuesday to determine your interest in arranging an appointment.

Conclude by showing your appreciation for being considered. This formal thank you can be stated in a number of ways:

> Thank you for considering my application. I wish you every success in filling this important and exciting position.

WHAT TO AVOID

Following are eight errors that weaken the effectiveness of a cover letter:

▸ *Blandness:* You need to catch your reader's attention, and using insipid and boring prose won't help you do that. Keep in mind that you are just one of dozens, if not hundreds, of applicants.

▷ *Rambling:* Don't ramble or provide too much information. You need to concentrate on the job and the match between an employer's needs and your credentials. You can, and should, inject a bit of your personality, but you certainly don't need to go into detail.

▷ *Excessive self-focus:* You must talk about yourself in a cover letter, but the employer or organization to which you are applying should always be your overriding focus.

▷ *Bad grammar, faulty punctuation, poor style, and typos:* As mentioned above, these are the kiss of death. If you make these mistakes, your application will simply be a waste of your time.

▷ *Conceit:* There is a fine line between explaining your potential worth and trumpeting your wonderfulness. Again, if you focus on the employer's needs, you will avoid the egocentricity that leads to bragging.

▷ *Self-deprecation:* A faint heart never won fair bride. If ever there was a place to be assertive about what you can offer an organization, it's in your cover letter and during your interview. Everyone understands that these are all about selling yourself. Timidity is not characteristic of good problem solvers.

▷ *Aggression:* Pushiness is rarely effective. Don't tell potential employers what they should or should not do. Don't provide them with the times that you'll be available for an interview.

▷ *Lengthiness:* One-page letters are best. Spilling over to a second page is acceptable if your letter is well written, but most of that page should remain blank.

A sample cover letter appears in Appendix 2 at the end of this chapter. If you were hiring, would it encourage you to contact the applicant for an interview?

Networking and the information interview

Don't let the number of books and businesses devoted to resumes and cover letters mislead you about the most important aspect of the job search. Networking is more effective than formally applying for advertised jobs, even if you have the world's greatest resume or cover letter. But what if you've spent most of your waking hours either studying or working at a part-time job and have absolutely zero networking experience? Where do you begin?

Fortunately, there's a well-established and universally understood mechanism for networking called the information interview. This is a brief question-and-answer session with someone who works in a job or for an organization that interests you.

That person is not a manager or someone who has the authority to hire you. Rather, it is an individual who enjoys his or her work and is willing to spend a few minutes talking to you about it. This form of interview is pressure-free for both participants, and it features lots of shared enthusiasm. It also enables you to start creating a network.

Arranging information interviews is relatively easy. Most professionals are familiar with them and are happy to talk about their work. Your professors can probably give you at least one name. You can also find people at LinkedIn, at on-line e-mail directories, or via an Internet search. Look for people with whom you have something in common: your program, school, or some other characteristic.

Once you have a name, send an e-mail, or call, to ask the person for ten minutes at her convenience. Let her know that your sole interest is learning about her job, and make it clear that there are no strings attached. Busy professionals commonly feel pressured by the demands of their workload, so assure her that you will take no more than ten minutes.

Dress appropriately. This meeting is informal, so you probably don't need to wear a suit, tie, and all the other trappings of an official interview. Take your cue from the way in which professionals in the field dress at work. If in doubt, lean toward the dressy rather than the casual.

Some people feel that they cannot be themselves in formal attire. That is a very foolish and self-defeating attitude. Most professions have a dress code, even if it allows a range of choices. Individuals who work in professions are no less unique simply because they conform to an accepted standard.

Arrive early. This shows that you respect the time of your interviewee. Adhere strictly to the ten-minute schedule.

Bring a notepad and take notes. This reveals that you are serious about what you'll learn. Ask the following questions:

- Why did you choose your profession?
- How did you get your first job after graduating from university?
- What do you like most about your work?
- What do you like least about it?
- If you could give just one piece of advice to someone who is considering entering your profession, what would it be?
- Might you give me the names and contact information of other people who would speak to me about the profession?
- May I use your name when I contact them?

Don't be surprised if the meeting lasts much longer than ten minutes, at the insistence of the interviewee. After all, who doesn't like to talk about him- or herself? However, remain alert for signals that the session is over, and leave as soon as you notice them.

AFTER THE INFORMATION INTERVIEW

The first task after an information interview is to thank the interviewee for her valuable time. When you get home, put her name on an index card, or create a computer file, and add a few comments about the meeting. While it's still fresh in your mind, compose and send a thank you note to the interviewee, either via e-mail or a posted greeting card.

Now begin creating your network. By following up on the leads from your interviewee, you will soon have a list of contacts in the profession. Always contact everyone. You will click better with some than with others and will feel comfortable approaching them again. Congratulations! You've begun to build a network.

Keep your network warm. Be careful not to bother your contacts. But if you interview someone whom they suggested, don't hesitate to send an e-mail to let them know how it went. Because professional networks are complex and overlapping, you will continually find that interviewees know each other. This gives you another chance to send an e-mail. Some of your contacts will use your visit as an opportunity to call or renew contact with someone else on your list. Over time, your name will become known and your interest in the profession will be documented.

The greatest benefit of your network is that you will learn when jobs come up. Most jobs (the majority) are never advertised. The only way to learn of them is through your network. Typically, one of your contacts will let you know if an employment opportunity arises.

When this occurs, check your network to

- determine whether the position is right for you
- seek advice on how best to apply for it
- discover what major problems the organization faces
- learn who does the hiring and whether contacting him or her is appropriate. Making contact, rather than simply entering the hiring process, greatly multiplies your chance of success.

NETWORKING AT UNIVERSITY

Don't expect a fully functional network to appear overnight. Unless you have an inside track, several months will usually elapse before it begins to produce fruit in terms of tips and opportunities. People who change careers report that building a network in their new field takes about four to six months.

The best possible practice is to start at university. Ask your professors or teaching assistants for the names of contacts (such as former students). Attend on-campus lectures on topics of interest and try to get to know the speakers. If you have guest speakers in your classes, talk to them for a few minutes after their presentation. Get their business card. Contact them later. They might not recall your name, but they will be pleased that a student remembers them and wants more information.

Conducting research for an essay or presentation provides an ideal opportunity to make contacts and obtain information. Courses with a placement component are an excellent means to create a network. To wait until after graduation to start looking for work simply wastes the opportunities at school. Moreover, if you start early and keep your network warm over a period of years rather than months, it will be grounded in more genuine, and hence effective, relationships.

STARTING AND ENERGIZING YOUR NETWORK

Many professional associations accept student members. For example, the Institute of Public Administration of Canada has special memberships for students who are interested in working for government. For the modest sum of fifty-five dollars, students get access to the institute's publications and will be invited to professional events, some designed especially for them and for new professionals.

Joining a professional association as a student is a great way to start a network and learn outside the classroom. The investment of money and time is small, but the rewards can be immense.

You can also boost your network by writing for local newspapers and Internet-only publications, which are always looking for new and timely material (especially if it's free!). Consider composing a short article of three to five hundred words on something interesting or a hot topic that relates to your studies or extracurricular interests. Including quotes from professors or professionals in your network will help to make the story more newsworthy.

Writing an article will get you noticed, provide a legitimate excuse for contacting people in your network, and result in a document that you can leave with them.

MISUSE OF INFORMATION INTERVIEWS

Every good thing is subject to abuse. Some individuals disingenuously exploit information interviews as job-hunting mechanisms. Employers and professionals resent being used in this way. It is critical, therefore, that you are honestly seeking information about a professional career in which you are genuinely interested. It's equally important not to use the interview as a way of getting others to do your job search for you. Finally, never use the interview as a deceitful way of accessing someone whom you hope will give you a job.

NETWORKING AND MENTORING

As your career advances, you will still need the support of your network and must keep it viable. As career advisors put it, you need to keep it warm. For some individuals, this will become second nature, whereas for others it's a chore that must be scheduled.

Remember that a network works both ways. In time, university students may start to ask you for information interviews. Treat them well, and remember that what goes around, comes around. They will help keep your network warm as they contact the people whom you recommend to them.

The real interview

In *What Color Is Your Parachute?* the best job-hunting book, Richard Bolles estimates that 98 percent of applicants go into job interviews like sheep to the slaughter. The sheep fail to understand that interviews are all about sizing each other up to see if there is a good match.

This sizing-up process is a lot like dating. You should be yourself but on your very best behaviour. You wouldn't reveal everything about yourself on a first date, would you? You'd listen as much as talk, wouldn't you? You'd want to ensure that your first date wasn't your last. The same is true of an interview.

Interviews are governed by certain conventions, which you need to follow:

▸ Wear formal attire. It doesn't matter what makes you comfortable. Interviewers expect you to dress appropriately for a professional interview.
▸ Arrive about ten minutes early. This indicates that you can schedule yourself well and that you respect the time of the interviewer.
▸ If you're offered tea or coffee, the right answer is "No, thank you." Sipping coffee while being interviewed is not professional.
▸ Open your notepad and be prepared to take notes. This demonstrates that you are an active listener and helps to answer questions. Record the names of the people who are interviewing you. This will help you remember their names throughout the meeting, and after.
▸ Trained interviewers may begin by making light conversation to make you feel comfortable. Recognize this for what it is, and don't

be tempted to relax. Be aware that a complex interaction is about to occur. Again, think of a date, and you won't be far off.

▸ Most interview questions have a hidden meaning. These will be discussed later on. Many probe for problems in your past or your personality that might make you unsuitable.

▸ Interviewers are alert for hints that you may be unmotivated, lazy, unenthusiastic, arrogant, irresponsible, whiny, uncollegial, indiscreet, or unethical, or that you have problems with authority. Therefore, your responses must avoid sending any signals of these undesirable traits.

On the positive side, the employer is looking for signs that you can fit in, learn, and apply the skills you acquired at university. Your task is to provide as much information as possible to demonstrate your maturity, responsibility, collegiality, and good communication and critical skills.

You are expected to make good eye contact. It's advisable to smile but not to joke, be ironic, sarcastic, witty, or anything else that might detract from your professionalism. Many of those behaviours signal a potentially problematic personality.

Bring extra copies of your resume and cover letter, your best university essays, your transcripts, and other documents from school or your past/current job. You may not need them all, but being able to provide evidence of your accomplishments will boost your confidence. If you are not asked for them, you can still – if appropriate – offer to leave a copy behind. Doing so will set you apart from other applicants and give the interviewers something to remember you by.

Typically, near the end of the session, you will be asked whether you have questions. If you don't, you've squandered a wonderful opportunity to show knowledge of, and interest in, the organization. You've probably also given the impression that you're too passive.

Your self-possession, intelligence, and professionalism are always under the microscope, whether it's evident or not. Some interviews are grilling sessions; some seem to be a walk in the park. Don't be misled by either. Keep your composure and a positive attitude, even if you think your interviewer hates you. You might be pleasantly surprised.

By the same token, just because the interview was a pleasant experience, it doesn't mean that the job is yours. Be realistic. Just because your first date went well, it doesn't mean that you'll be getting a marriage proposal, or even a second date.

You can learn a lot from television programs such as *The Bachelor* and *The Bachelorette*. The nicest or best-looking contestant doesn't always win the prize. Sometimes the prize isn't even worth the effort, as some successful players discovered afterward. At the same time, it's easy to spot people who screw up the dating game by giving too much away too early, by being too needy, or by sending signals that they just might belong in a padded cell!

Interviewers are usually on a tight schedule, so don't be surprised if the session ends abruptly. You may feel dismissed when this occurs, but it's very important to retain your composure, rise quickly, shake hands, express your brief and courteous thanks, and leave. Don't throw in any last comments, or say how much you like the organization, or whatever. It's over; get the hell out!

EXCEPTIONS

There are exceptions to every rule, of course. Some of your interviewers may not follow these rituals at all. They may decide to hire you precisely because you were sarcastic, or wore sneakers, or displayed an aggressive personality. But don't bet on it. By not adhering to the rules, you send the message that you might be a problem. The last thing a manager wants is a potential problem.

Think about it. Recruiting a university graduate costs an organization much time and money. But getting rid of someone who doesn't blend in is far more costly. As a result, employers almost always play it safe when selecting a new worker.

In general, regardless of the interview situation, it is best to err on the side of conservatism. Don't display your full personality. The interview is neither the time nor the place for complete disclosure.

THE THANK YOU LETTER OR E-MAIL

All things being equal, those who send a thank you note or e-mail after the interview have a much better chance of getting the position than those who don't. Moreover, this is the right place to touch on material that wasn't addressed during the interview.

A thank you letter or e-mail should never be more than two or three short paragraphs. It usually remains unread, but that doesn't detract from its usefulness. What will be remembered is that you took the time to write and send it. You will find a sample thank you letter in Appendix 3 at the end of this chapter.

Decoding interview questions

As with writing exams, the key to a successful interview is understanding the questions. Below, we decode many of the questions that are asked during an interview:

1 Tell us about yourself.

Translation: Here's some rope. Want to hang yourself?

Explanation: People who ask this question are looking for potential problems that you might bring with you. They are also curious about your self-image. What do you think about you?

Solution: Your task here is to suggest that you are a reliable person with a good employment record who has profited from being in university, not to blurt out your life. You can answer this question constructively by quoting some positive comments from your employers, teachers, or references.

Duration: Two minutes, tops.

2 Why did you apply for this job?

Variation: What kind of work are you looking for?

Translation: Show us how you fit our precise needs.

Explanation: Obviously, your interviewers know far more than you do about the position to be filled. Their question asks you to explain what you want from the job before you even know the particulars. If your description doesn't match theirs, you can be eliminated.

Solution: If you know exactly what they're looking for (through your network or due to your study of the organization), show them that you are precisely what they need. If not, turn the question around and ask for more details about the job itself. Say something like, "I'd love to talk about my suitability for the position, but perhaps you could give me some more information about what it specifically involves."

Duration: Up to ten minutes. This is the heart of the interview.

3 What experience/expertise do you have in this line of work?

Variation: What makes you think you'd be good at this job?

Translation: You don't seem to have much experience. You probably can't do this job.

Explanation: Candidates who are entering the professional marketplace and don't yet have the experience that many employers want can count on being asked this question.

Solution: Don't apologize for your lack of experience or say that you're willing to learn. That just makes you look needy. Demonstrate that you have transferable skills, including your professionalism, that can be applied to the position. Finally, remind them that you've mastered many things in the past and will do so in the future.

Duration: Up to ten minutes. This is where you sell yourself.

4 Can you describe an example of how you handled a difficult situation involving other people?

Variation: How did you get along with previous employers or co-workers?

Translation: Prove to us that you are not difficult to get along with.

Explanation: All employment positions are based on collaboration and teamwork. Thus, hiring someone who can work with others is far better than engaging a brilliant individual who is hard to get along with, especially for entry-level jobs. If interviewers suspect that you might be difficult, they'll cross you off their list.

This question can have several layers that will become apparent as the session progresses. Interviewers also look for a tendency to criticize employers or fellow workers. To indulge in this behaviour is to shoot yourself in the foot. If you do it during an interview, when you're on your best behaviour, chances are that you'll do it again, and even more frequently, on the job.

Interviewers may push you into discussing a serious conflict with an employer, co-worker, or teacher. Since almost everyone who has ever breathed on the planet will have at least one bad relationship, you cannot avoid this trap.

Solution: Describe an employment situation in which you acted maturely to get people on your side or to defuse conflict. Always emphasize the strong qualities that you demonstrated in resolving clashes and the positives that you took from difficult people and situations.

If you're asked for details, don't hesitate to provide them. Just remember to deal with them maturely and to present them as a learning experience. Find ways of saying nice things about the people who were involved. Never trash talk even the most irritating individuals or their actions. This will simply make you look bad. Your purpose in the interview is to show that you are above any pettiness, even if you've clearly been wronged. Haven't we all? It's how we deal with it that counts.

Duration: This can take anywhere from ten to fifteen minutes, depending on the depth of probing.

5 Can you explain the gap in your work-school history?

Variations: Why did you take a year out between high school and university? Why did it take you five years to complete a four-year program? What did you do during the year that isn't mentioned in your resume?

Translation: Are you a quitter, a failure, a slacker?

Explanation: Employment gaps used to be the biggest black spots on a resume. In the current job market, employers expect more transitions and view changes more positively than in the past. But gaps still provide them with an opportunity to investigate.

Solution: Your task is to show that you are dedicated to your work. You took time out *because* you are serious – it helped you to prepare for a challenge or renew your skills. You used the gap time to become a better person and a better employee. Assure the interviewers that you will make a serious commitment to the job (at least five years).

Duration: Five minutes, tops.

6 Tell us about a problem that you solved in life, school, or at work.

Variation: Have you ever experienced a serious problem in your life? How did you solve it?

Translation: Prove to us that you are a problem solver.

Explanation: This is a positive question. It attempts to discover whether you've acquired the critical skills that we explore throughout this book. Employers want to hire people who can identify little problems before they become major headaches and who can discover creative solutions.

One of the biggest disappointments to an employer is the passive employee who does his or her job reasonably well but who does not otherwise contribute to the survival and success of the organization. To find a person who will solve problems while not adding to an organization's existing difficulties is the goal of every good interviewer.

Solution: You can't answer this question well unless you have developed your critical skills. Contrived answers are fairly easy to spot, and further inquiry will merely expose more fundamental weaknesses. At the same time, a good answer requires some preparation before the interview. Think about problems and challenges in your past and how you dealt with them. If you could have handled them better, say so, and explain how you would respond to them today.

You can use examples from your studies in replying to this (and other) questions. Perhaps you were stuck in a group project with someone who failed to contribute. How did you deal with this? How would you cope with a similar problem in the workplace?

The point here is to demonstrate that you can both identify problems and work logically and creatively toward their solution. You also want to show that you can think both laterally and vertically in the process. If some of your most original solutions resulted from working in tandem with others, so much the better.

The ability to mix creativity and collaboration with problem solving can't help but impress your interviewers.

Duration: Up to ten minutes.

7 What is your greatest weakness?

Variation: What personal qualities do you feel you need to work on to be a better person or employee?

Translation: Tell us what's wrong with you so that we can reject you immediately.

Explanation: This question usually comes near the end, when you are getting just a bit tired or cocky. It's a serious trap and its purpose is solely to eliminate you as a candidate. It's the question from hell – unless you're prepared for it.

Honest but inexperienced candidates are often lured in by this question, especially if they feel that the interview has gone well and that they have a good feeling about the interviewer. It doesn't matter how nice the interviewer is, this question is part of the standard repertoire, and its intent is to identify flaws. Uninformed honesty is not the best policy here.

Solution: Fortunately, no one is perfect. In fielding this question, provide a weakness that also counts as a strength. Saying something like, "I have a tendency to work a little too hard when I'm completing an interesting project" never lost anyone a job. You can even make a weakness work for you, by saying, "I'm a person who likes to take the initiative and to do more than is expected. This means that I occasionally get irritated if I'm being supervised too closely." If you get the job, your supervisor will probably give you more freedom than usual.

Duration: Five minutes, tops.

8 Where do you expect to be in your career in five years' time?

Variation: How do you want your career to develop?

Translation: Are you just looking for a paycheque, or do you want a meaningful career?

Explanation: Employers want to know whether you are a good investment. Will you grow with the organization and into successively responsible positions? That would be their ideal.

The five-year specification is a meaningful one. In many professions, it's understood that people may jump to other organizations after five years as a way of advancing their careers. Moving up is sometimes easier to achieve by moving on than by staying in one place. You need to know this, if only because interviewers are aware of it.

Solution: Show that you are reasonably ambitious, which means doing some research on your career and its probable trajectory. You want to convey that you thrive on challenges and opportunities but without giving the impression that you'll set the office on its ear. You want to look like someone who will grow and develop in your career.

In five years, you want to have improved your professional skills to the point that your employer will recognize your growth and place you in an appropriate position. The implication can be that you will seek those challenges elsewhere if they were not forthcoming from your organization. But you should never say this explicitly, or your commitment might come into question.

Duration: Up to five minutes.

9 What are your salary expectations?

Variation: What was your salary in your previous job?

Translation: Can we afford you?

Explanation: Your potential cost is always on the employer's mind during the interview, especially if you are an impressive candidate with specialized degrees and experience. Although interviewers know that asking about salary is unprofessional at this stage, they often fish for the information anyway because it helps them decide between equally good contenders.

Also, they know that you'll be in a much better bargaining position once they've offered you the job. If you fall into the trap of agreeing to salary now rather than waiting until you're presented with a contract, you'll make their lives easier.

Solution: You never know what kind of pressure you'll encounter during an interview. For this reason, it's a good idea to have a salary range in mind that is based on the statistical averages for your profession. But it is important not to negotiate salary unless your hand is forced.

Simply explain that you cannot discuss it unless a formal offer of employment has been made and you are seriously considering it. Right now, you'd prefer to concentrate on the issue at hand, which is discovering whether your skills match their needs.

Upon being offered the job, you'll enter into the salary negotiation and will be able to leverage the highest possible wage at that time. Once they make their choice, they won't want to start interviewing again. Be prepared to be reasonable, but also remember that getting higher pay is much easier when you are being recruited or hired than after you are in place.

Duration: Under normal conditions, this question should be dealt with in less than a minute, since you do not want to commit at this time.

10 Do you have any questions for us?

Variation: Is there anything that you'd like to tell us?

Translation: This is your opportunity to size us up.

Explanation: Most of the interview is structured around their questions and your responses. A skilful candidate will have compiled a list of questions before the interview and will ask them where appropriate. The rule of thumb for a good interview is that interviewer and interviewee each talk for 50 percent of the time. This is a clear sign of matchmaking, where two individuals are feeling each other out and engaging in a courtship ritual.

Depending on the nature of the interview, this may not be possible. If many people need to be interviewed, or if there is more than one interviewer, your questions may be left to the end of the session.

Even if the interviewers are not particularly interested in your questions, they will expect you to have some. Failing to ask questions implies either neediness, lack of interest, or insufficient research on the position and the organization.

Solution: Show that you've done your homework by asking about the job or the organization. Highlighting an issue or problem that it, the industry, or the profession is facing and then seeking your interviewers' opinion is always very effective. Make the most of this opportunity to show off your knowledge and interest.

Your questions should not be focused on yourself. It's fine to ask for clarification of some aspects of the position or to elaborate on an earlier answer, but demonstrating your interest in them rather than your needs or desires is most effective here. This approach works well in dating and in job hunting.

Duration: Variable, but prepare a good ten minutes of questions, even if the responses are abbreviated. Here are ten questions to ask at the formal interview:

1 Can you describe a typical day on the job?
2 What are your organization's three top goals for the coming year?
3 What are the biggest challenges in this position?
4 What are the major challenges facing your organization?
5 What are the career opportunities for someone who excels in this position?
6 What is your organization's management style or philosophy?
7 How do you rank this position in terms of the organization's bottom line?
8 What kinds of people succeed best in this organization?
9 What kinds of people have not succeeded in this organization?
10 What is your ideal employee?

ON-CAMPUS SERVICES AND INTERVIEWS

Your university or college probably has a career preparation office or service. You would be wise to visit it and see what it offers. You may find much or little, but it is crucial to check. However, finding the ideal job is largely a do-it-yourself project. Your university and program can give you the tools, but you must wield them yourself to get a job.

Some employers conduct on-campus interviews that tend to be coordinated by the career services/placement office. Signing up for these will encourage you to prepare your resume and, if offered an interview, to practise your interview skills.

INTERVIEWS AT SMALL COMPANIES

Much of the advice above is tailored to large organizations with trained human resources personnel. However, small companies are creating many new jobs these days, and here the interviewer will also be the employer. This has its pros and cons for a job hunter.

On the positive side, you'll probably be interviewed by the person who does the hiring and who will make the decision quickly. On the other hand, he or she probably won't be trained in interviewing. Human resources professionals have considerable expertise at putting people at their ease and discovering their potential.

Untrained interviewers are often nervous and uncomfortable when screening candidates. They can also be insensitive, and occasionally offensive, even if unintentionally. In these situations, many of the rituals outlined above won't apply, and your strategy should change accordingly.

Here's what you need to remember for interviews by the owner of a small company or organization:

- He or she is probably just as nervous as you are.
- You are responsible for ensuring that the right questions are asked.
- Putting the interviewer at ease is critical.
- Following up after the session is even more critical, since the interviewer probably won't have a good basis for making a decision.
- Don't be hard on yourself if you don't get the job. The interview was good practice, and there will be many more opportunities if you are scouting small companies.
- Try to add the employer to your network. There's a good chance that she or he will hire the wrong person and may be looking for someone in the future.

In many respects, small companies are the ideal environments for personal growth because they are less bureaucratic and provide many more opportunities to develop your professional skills.

The smaller companies cannot invest as heavily in recruitment and must therefore rely more on networking to find employees. They are also much more likely to accept non-traditional working relationships.

Overall, you should be thinking about the opportunities being created by small innovative businesses. For people who are just starting out, these companies may be the best places to break in and obtain professional experience.

Interview styles

Although the interview tips we have provided here will work most of the time, some organizations have opted for very different ways of conducting an interview.

THE CONVERSATIONAL APPROACH

Here, the interviewer engages the candidate in conversation rather than asking direct questions. The probing is done in such a relaxed and casual manner that it is easy to be caught off guard and reveal too much information. The key here is to remember the rules for performing well in an interview and never to drop your professional guard.

THE CONSENSUS APPROACH

Because recruiting and retaining good employees costs so much, many organizations have adopted a team approach to interviewing, on the grounds that several heads are better than one when it comes to selecting a new employee. These interviews can be daunting because the candidate must deal with several people whose personalities sometimes conflict.

In this situation, you can't possibly control the variables as well as in a one-on-one interview. The secret here is to practise good listening skills (active listening!) and take notes. This enables you to pick up on the subtext of someone's question while maintaining good eye contact and rapport with the entire team.

Taking your time in answering questions is the most important thing you can do here. If someone suspects that you are nervous and tries to help, just gently inform him that you are thinking about the best way to address the question.

Although consensus interviews can seem stressful, performing well in them is actually a lot easier than in the one-on-one version with a skilled interviewer. The scrutiny is far less deep, and the differences among the team give you lots more time to pay attention to the dynamics.

THE STRESS APPROACH

A new kind of interviewing style is to subject the candidate to stress. This is often accomplished by a variety of boorish techniques, such as making highly controversial statements and demanding an immediate reply or responding to a candidate's questions or answers with prolonged silence.

The effectiveness of this approach is highly questionable. It's grounded in the assumption that because the modern world is a hectic place, the best employees are those who can deal with stress. There might be some validity in this, were it not for the fact that the stress interview is relatively easy to master. The strategy for coping is to keep your cool, calmly deflect uncomfortable questions, defuse controversial statements by reinterpreting them in a professional manner, and aim for a balanced and judicious response, despite the tone or aggression of the interviewers.

Since the whole point of a stress interview is to determine whether you buckle under pressure, all you need to do is stay calm.

ALL-DAY AND RESTAURANT INTERVIEWS

Some organizations like to spend an entire day or at least an extended meal with potential employees. The idea here is that, whereas candidates may manage to hide their true personality during a short interview, it will come out in the course of a busy day or an evening meal. This reasoning is debatable, but if you end up in an interview like this, there are some things that you need to know.

Your stomach is potentially your worst enemy during these extended negotiations. During an all-day interview, you need to keep the blood flowing to your brain rather than your tummy, so carry a good supply of nutritious snacks in case you get hungry. Give alcohol a pass at the restaurant interview. The only good thing about this form of interview is that you won't be expected to pay for the food.

THE SECOND AND THIRD INTERVIEWS

The creation of successive interviews is one sign of just how seriously large organizations take the hiring process. It used to be that one was enough. These days, however, even three interviews are sometimes seen as insufficient, and hopeful candidates may find themselves going through a roller-coaster ride of sessions that may take many weeks.

This provides some very good reasons for relaxing about the process. There's no point in getting worked up about a position that involves several interviews with various people. It's not healthy. Plus, the gap between the first and third interviews gives you time to reflect on the nature of the organization and whether it's right for you.

Experienced job hunters never put all their eggs in one basket. Instead, they apply for several jobs at the same time. That way, if they don't land one of them, they can immediately turn their thoughts to other opportunities rather than brooding about the one that got away.

References

In most occupations, you are not expected to submit your references when you apply for a position. It's uncommon, and even unprofessional, to request them at that point. You may be asked to supply them at the interview, but most times, potential employers will deal with references only once a candidate is being seriously considered. They may ask for a formal letter, or they may be content with an e-mailed reference.

Choosing references carefully is critical because employers place significant value on what they reveal about you. With one exception, discussed below, never give someone as a reference without getting his or her approval first. Also, describe the job that you are applying for. Be sure that the person is comfortable in the role of referee; if not, find someone else.

Giving the name of a current employer as a reference can raise complex issues (disloyalty, for example). One approach is to provide the name, but with a request that your boss be contacted only if you are very seriously under consideration and that you be told first. This allows you to speak to your current employer only when he or she is about to be contacted.

Professors are good references for recent graduates or current students, since they are perceived to be impartial. If you click with a professor or two, don't hesitate to ask. However, remember that they sometimes take research trips (especially in the summer) and can't respond immediately to requests for references.

Typically, you'll be asked to provide three references. Aim for a mix: your current employer, a professor, a past employer, someone with whom you did volunteer work, and so forth.

Your three references should be formatted something like the examples below. Be sure to provide full contact information. It is acceptable to include very brief notes regarding your referees to help your interviewers identify their role in your life.

References for [insert your name]

Professor Thomas Klassen
Department of Political Science
York University
4700 Keele Street
Toronto, Ontario M3J 1P3
Voice: 416-736-2100 ext. 88828
E-mail: tklassen@yorku.ca

[In 2013-14, I took two half-year courses from Professor Klassen: one dealt with public policy, the other with research methods. Professor Klassen prefers to be contacted by e-mail.]

Ms. Simone Wisdom
Manager, Customer Complaints
xxx
xxx
xxx
Voice:
E-mail:

[Ms. Wisdom is my current employer.]

Mr. Markut Smart
Coordinator
xxx
xxx
xxx
Voice:
E-mail:

[Mr. Smart manages the community centre where I have volunteered for two years.]

After the interview

Be aware that some employers try to keep candidates on the hook while they make a decision or negotiate with the leading competitor. It's natural for them to look after their own self-interest, but it's equally important for you to look after yours. If they ask, as they often do, you can tell them that you are interviewing for other comparable positions. If they are reasonable, they will understand. If they are interested in you, this information may prompt them to act more quickly.

The wait after an interview can be lengthy and feel even lengthier. At this point, there's not much you can do, other than continue your job hunt and go to interviews. Getting depressed will not help.

You are in the labour market, and as in any market – whether it involves stocks, pork bellies, or oil – there must be a match between the seller (you) and the buyer (the employer). This will not occur immediately and probably not during your first attempt. Wait for a good match between the employment position and your interests and abilities.

Of course, counselling patience is easier than practising it. As you wait for replies from employers, stay in touch with your network and keep looking for other jobs. Things will work out!

Appendix 1: SAMPLE RESUMES

Terry Mah

113-320 Heathdale Street, Toronto, ON M7S 6R8
voice/fax: 416-987-5678
e-mail: t.mah@yorku.ca
web: mysiteatweebly.com

EDUCATION

Honours BA in History – York University, Toronto
graduating this June

- specializing in twentieth-century North American history, especially immigration and trade agreements
- GPA: *B average overall; B+ for history courses; A– for fourth-year courses*
- wrote an eighteen-page essay on Canada-US trade relations in the 1980s for a fourth-year course that earned a grade of A+ (the professor wrote, "this is a wonderful paper: original and very well researched").

BA in the Philosophy of Religion – Beijing University, China
2008-10 – incomplete

- majored in Buddhist philosophy, especially in East Asia (China, Korea, and Japan).

EMPLOYMENT

General Office Assistant – Kim and Associates, Accountants and Income Tax Experts, Toronto
2014-present (summer full-time; part-time during school year, six hours a week)

- learned basic bookkeeping principles and techniques in order to support the accounting team
- assist clients with various accounting and finance inquiries on the phone, in person, and via e-mail – such as confirming details of transactions and checking Canada Revenue Agency files
- refer complex inquiries and requests to the appropriate team member and follow up
- maintain a clean workspace and friendly professional atmosphere, including filing hard and soft documents, and ordering office supplies.

Front Desk Agent – Delta Chelsea Hotel, Toronto
2011-13 (full-time, summer, and part-time)

- settled and confirmed guest accounts on departure, often under time pressure, and with guests who did not speak English
- assisted in the training and supervision of new part-time staff, including teaching how to use booking reservation and financial software
- processed incoming and outgoing guests, including VIPs and airline staff, at a counter reserved for them.

Reservation Agent – Utell International
(an international travel-booking agency), Beijing Branch
2010-11 (full-time)

- arranged hotel reservations worldwide for Chinese business travellers, under tight deadlines, via e-mail and telephone
- investigated complaints from clients and resolved these with the hotels in Europe and Australia.

Researcher – China National Tourism Corporation, Beijing
2009 (summer)

- conducted short in-person interviews with departing international travellers at the Beijing and Shanghai airports.

VOLUNTEER

Gym Teacher – St. Ann's Public School, Toronto
2014-present (four hours on Saturdays)

- prepare weekly exercises for grade four and five students, including demonstrating first aid
- arrange for students to attend Toronto Maple Leaf hockey games, including raising funds from parents.

Student Ambassador – York University
2014-present (three hours a week)

- give prospective students and their parents tours of the university campus
- translate e-mail from Mandarin to English for delegations visiting from China
- direct visitors to events on campus and provide them information about the university.

Alex Menzies

Mail: 34 Hillcrest Ave, Anytown, MY L4S 2Y1
E-mail: Alex.Menzies@myuni.edu
Phone: 816-234-5678

EDUCATION

Bachelor of Arts, Business and Society
MY University, Anytown, 2014-

- expected graduation in May 2018
- B average in first year (five courses, including Psychology, History, and English)
- Sociology and Labour Studies stream.

WORK EXPERIENCE

Private Tutor (evenings)
Self-employed, My Town, 2012-13

- tutored grades ten and eleven students in English, French, and math
- motivated them by organizing weekly exercises and assignments, and providing constructive feedback
- responded to parent inquiries about their progress, including scheduling meetings to review progress.

Assistant Supervisor (full-time)
Tim Hortons, Next Town, 2011-12

- learned to resolve conflicts with customers and staff about service quality
- mainly managed energetic and inexperienced part-time staff
- developed loyal customer relationships by memorizing the names and preferences of regular customers.

Returns Clerk (full-time)
Nexten Warehouse, Any Town, 2010-12

- entered and retrieved product data in large electronic database
- conducted a daily physical inventory of returned products and logged this
- packed and labelled products to prevent damage and ensure safe transport.

INFORMATION TECHNOLOGY SKILLS

- expert in various software programs, including Microsoft Word, Microsoft Outlook, and Adobe Acrobat
- proficient in the use of spreadsheet programs, including Microsoft Excel and Lotus
- superior keyboarding skills, eighty words per minute.

OTHER SKILLS AND ACHIEVEMENTS

- fluent in French, reading knowledge of Hindi
- certified group fitness (aerobics) instructor with teaching experience
- volunteer experience with developmentally handicapped children aged eight to twelve.

Samantha Pereira

2600 White Road, Vancouver, BC V1Z 2X3
Telephone: (604) 234-5678
E-mail: sperreira@ubc.ca

EDUCATION

BA in Sociology, University of British Columbia –
completing first year of studies

EMPLOYMENT

CASHIER   **Safeway**
16-24 hours per week, 13 April 2013–14 December 2014

- provided friendly and patient customer service during peak
  times, without any transaction errors
- responsible for accurately knowing 245 product codes
- trained in theft control, including credit card and cheque fraud.

DAY CARE WORKER   **Self-employed**
3 days a week, 8 hours per day, 12 June 2013–13 September 2013

- cared responsibly for two children (aged 3 and 5) in their home
- prepared nutritional and balanced meals and snacks
- organized indoor and outdoor activities with the children.

PEER LEADER (volunteer)   **Vancouver Youth Outreach Service**
Drug and Alcohol Abuse Prevention, January 2013–13 June 2013

- assisted in the development of creative and interesting hard
  copy and Internet teaching materials with other volunteers
- accompanied volunteers to grades 9 and 10 high school
  classrooms to help demonstrate.

TUTOR (volunteer)   **Vancouver Public Library**
Homework Club, May 2011–June 2012

- assisted newly arrived immigrant students between the ages of
  8 and 11 with English-language homework
- created enriched learning materials for those who finished their
  homework.

Appendix 2: SAMPLE COVER LETTER

Andre Dawson
Any Street
My City, MY L4S 2Y1
Phone: 469-466-8945
E-mail: dawson@myuniversty.edu

28 January 2015

ABC Library Human Resources
Attention: Gloria Park
Manager of Circulation Services
ABC Library

Dear Ms. Park,

If you need someone with superior organizational skills and an ability to communicate effectively with different kinds of people in complex situations, I would like an opportunity to talk with you.

The attached resume describes someone who has studied at the MY University for two years and has a keen interest in working with diverse communities and with people from many backgrounds.

It highlights attention to detail, quality control, and processing skills that are major areas of responsibility for the Circulation Assistant position. And, hopefully, it describes someone that you would like to have working with you to ensure that services are provided in an efficient and friendly manner.

Although I have no experience working in a library, I have considerable knowledge of the book industry. In my current employment position, I have responsibility for purchasing and selling books.

Last summer, I volunteered for three months during evening and week-end hours at a children's reading program at a community centre near my home. In that role, I found age-appropriate reading material, both hard copy and electronic, and in English and other languages for new immigrants.

I look forward to talking with you about how I could contribute to the effective functioning and welcoming atmosphere of the circulation desk.

I trust you will not mind if I e-mail or call early next week.

Sincerely yours,

Andre Dawson

resume attached

Appendix 3: SAMPLE THANK YOU LETTER

Bryan Baytes
24 Homewood Ave
My City, MY L4S 2Y1
Phone: 874-378-2355
E-mail: B.Baytes@uni.edu

15 April 2015

Sabrina Makhamra
Summer Programs Manager
Happy Summer Camps

Dear Ms. Makhamra:

It was a delight to meet you yesterday and learn more about Happy Summer Camps. I appreciate the time you spent showing me the impressive camp facilities and reviewing the responsibilities of the summer coordinator position.

During our conversation, you stressed the summer coordinator's important role of training counsellors. You may be assured that my education program at university and previous summer camp positions, specifically as assistant staff supervisor last summer at Lakeview Camp, have prepared me for the coordinator position.

Thank you once again for your time and consideration. I'm excited about the possibility of making this summer the best one ever for both the staff and children at Happy Summer Camps.

I look forward to hearing from you.

Sincerely,

Bryan Baytes

CHAPTER 10
Managing Social Media

In an age of constant live connections, the central question
of self-examination is drifting from "Who are you?" towards
"What are you doing?"

— Tom Chatfield, *How to Thrive in the Digital Age*

Arguably, nothing has blurred the relationship between the private self and the public domain more than the Internet. In the past, the "private" had something of a sacred quality that government, employers, professions, and colleagues did not seek to invade. Thanks in large part to social media, the private has become public.

We suggest that you confront the problems and opportunities of social media head-on. You can't be as effective as possible as a student, an employee, or even a friend or lover, unless you embrace social media.

By social media, we mean the creation and exchange of ideas and information via the Internet. Facebook, Twitter, Tumblr, wikis, blogs, YouTube, virtual game-worlds, and much else constitute social media. We all know people who seem content to allow Facebook, Twitter, Instagram, and computer simulations and trends to define parts of who they are and what they want from life. These individuals don't make good students, employees, or friends. They don't understand the difference between using tools and techniques and being the tool of someone, or something, else.

A sensible strategy is to embrace the valuable aspects of the borderless world without being overwhelmed by it. Use Internet communication in ways that allow *you* to develop a unique and authentic identity. Make your own choices.

Professor Dwyer is something of a techno-peasant. He has never owned a cellphone; he is not on Facebook; he disdains Twitter. Nonetheless, he can't escape the Internet. His students prefer to communicate with him by e-mail, and his university insists that he has an on-line presence. His teaching requires the use of webpages. At least he has some control over the information that flows from those sites.

Five rules for social media

The Internet sends out many signs and signals about us, over which we have little or no control. Anything that we say or do is potentially damaging information. For example, if you visit the website ratemyprofessor.com, you'll learn all kinds of things about Professor Dwyer that he doesn't want you to know. Years from now, Professor Dwyer will be dead and buried, but there's a good chance that his students' comments on his intelligence, teaching, and looks will still be alive and well on the Internet – and available for anyone to read.

Professor Dwyer is old (sixty-five), and he enjoys the luxury of mostly ignoring Internet messages about him. Presumably, you are not as old as he is (condolences if you are), so you need to take the opportunities and pitfalls of the Internet and social media into account in shaping your career as a student and beyond. The first and most important rule when dealing with social media is to assume that nothing is private and that information about you will be used in ways that you cannot control.

The second rule is that you have the power and responsibility to ensure that negative messages never reach the Internet in the first place. Better still, replace them with positive ones that you control. A useful activity is to search the Internet for your name. What do you find? How will others interpret any posts, tweets, photos, or other material that they find on-line?

Third, remind yourself that the erosion of privacy has an upside. Increasingly, public discourse pushes us out of self-imposed isolation; communication networks encourage positive relationship building and networking that compensates for the lack of privacy. As we suggest later in this chapter, you can use social media to your advantage at school, in your career, and in your life.

Fourth, the Internet is a superhighway, which means that it's crowded. Every minute is rush hour, and people lose their cool and honk at each other. Social media favour the few who have the critical and creative skills to sift through the shit and discover what isn't. If you choose your routes carefully and stay cool, the ride will be smoother and more adventurous.

Fifth, if a problem arises on social media, or if you screw up, take action right away. Suppose you sent an e-mail or posted a comment or photo that you soon regretted. The instinctive reaction is to wait and see, but this will compound the problem. Don't wait – apologize immediately to everyone who might be affected. Take ownership of the situation.

An apology might read as follows: "Dear Susan, I'm sorry for the inappropriate message I sent you a few minutes ago. It was written in haste and sent without editing. Please be assured that I did not intend to question your competency or your valuable contribution to the project. I am copying this e-mail to all group members to inform them of my apology."

Apologies need not be long, but they must be sincere and timely. Also try to apologize face-to-face. Do not transform the apology into an explanation: "I was tired and overloaded this morning, and also dealing with an urgent request ..."

If someone posts your photo on-line, you are entirely within your rights to ask that it be removed. If someone tags you in a photo or a post, you can almost always remove the tag yourself.

Social media and relationship building

Successful careers have always depended on networking and relationship building. Social media can help create and adapt networks. Failing to take advantage of this is to do yourself a disservice. As we noted in the previous chapter, social media makes it easier to build up a network of contacts, and to arrange information interviews.

The pervasiveness of e-mail, Facebook, and other messaging services is a case in point. E-mail can sometimes be a pain, but it is absolutely essential to doing business and getting results in the modern world. The minute you send a message, you are engaging in conversation with another person; in other words, you are entering into a relationship that could either help or hurt you in terms of what you want to do or where you want to go. Exercise care whenever you send a message because every single message is either a relationship builder or breaker.

For example, university students rely heavily on e-mail in connecting with their professors and teaching assistants. Many students are so accustomed to instant gratification that they automatically expect it. This is especially true at the beginning of an academic term: "Professor, is your course easy or hard?" "I can't find the required book in the bookstore. What should I do?!" "I want to switch my tutorial." "I was sick; did I miss anything important?" "I need your help!" "Your immediate response is requested."

These messages often lack a name at the bottom, a student number, or a reference to the specific course in question. Sometimes they come from non-university e-mail accounts. The spelling and punctuation are awful, suggesting that they were flung together without a moment's thought. They end up in the delete folder. In their search for immediate satisfaction, what students often forget is that communication is a two-way street.

Students who demand instantaneous information from teachers negate the relationship-building potential of e-mail. A polite request from a student who identifies him- or herself and the course constructs a positive image in the mind of the recipient. Good grammar and punctuation, and concise language, signal that the message was composed with care. An indication that the student has done some research – "I asked the bookstore staff about when additional copies of the book would arrive, but they did not know" – shows initiative. A short thank you for the information received consolidates that positive image.

In the workforce, only the foolish, the enraged, or the reckless would dare to send a rude electronic message. It can be forwarded to anyone, anywhere, at any time, and it remains in a folder long after a spoken comment has been forgotten.

A dominant, and to our minds quite toxic, thread in the fabric of e-mail communication is self-protection. Do you save e-mails that you've sent? Is this to prove you've not made a mistake, or that others did? The point of this hoarding exercise is to avoid blame. Those who insist first and foremost on protecting themselves are either very poor employees or are unlucky enough to work in a poisonous environment that they should consider leaving.

Another thread puts appearance over substance. Often e-mail messages are a request for assistance, a fact that has motivated some employees to become experts at *seeming* to be helpful. After giving a semi-legitimate reason for not offering their aid, they end with something like, "If there's anything I can do to help, just let me know." Those who constantly avoid contributing to the success of others will eventually discover that no one is willing to help them.

Of course, you need to protect yourself from those who would unfairly assign blame. And refusing to help is sometimes the right response, but adopting such techniques as a substitute for working with others and contributing to the success of a group or organization is self-defeating.

Many unhappy scenarios begin with a simple e-mail communication. Many positive relationships can develop if you treat e-mail as an engagement with other people.

Consider the nature of your electronic messages at work or at school. Do they reflect positive, optimistic, organized, and energized qualities – the kind of qualities that people find appealing?

Branding yourself

Your on-line presence is notable and permanent because information is rarely ever completely erased from the Internet. It's your job to project and protect a positive self-image on-line. This means never putting silly or salacious images and comments on the Internet.

Believe us, a prospective employer or mate will eventually discover these lapses in judgment, with the result that you'll be dismissed from serious consideration. In some instances, you might be able to exercise damage control, but the wisest strategy is to avoid making the mistake in the first place.

To use the language of business, everyone, whether he or she likes it, is a brand. Even if you have no on-line presence whatsoever, that is a negative brand. It may communicate that you have accomplished nothing, are a hermit, or lack the skills required for social media. The image that you send (or don't send) into the world may not be the real or the complete you, but it is you as the world sees you. That's why you should be diligent in developing and promoting your on-line brand.

Now, this doesn't mean transforming yourself into a marketer. Rather, we encourage you to construct a virtual version of yourself that will help you achieve your goals in school, work, and life.

A simple way of doing this is to establish your own website. A well-designed webpage, which is easily created from free software at Weebly.com, helps you to control the messages that you send out. At the cost of a few hours, you'll have a site that potential employers and others can visit.

Moreover, it can be the central location for information about you, including your resume. You can post your essays (after all, they are your work) and anything else that you've done: photos, art, a video of you reciting a poem for an English course – anything. However, remember that everything you post must be carefully selected.

In marketing yourself, never make the mistake of thinking that the "sizzle is more important than the steak." But there is no reason why your webpage can't display some of that sizzle. Be creative.

When you offer your resume to a prospective employer, it's wise to be traditional because many recruiters are suspicious of anything flashy. Similarly, applications for scholarships and graduate studies should err toward the conservative side. But a webpage allows you more scope in developing your image and has the additional benefit of demonstrating your proficiency with multimedia.

Although your page should be clean, crisp, and professional, you can also add hypertext links to take your readers in more unconventional directions if they so choose. Use them to showcase your skills and passions.

The most critical piece of advice in creating your webpage is to keep everything upbeat, hopefully without looking like a naive optimist. You want to avoid negativity, even if you think it's clever, sophisticated, and urbane. A corollary of this is that, if you link to other websites, ensure that they too avoid negativity – you can always be damned by association.

A personal website is an exceptionally powerful tool. Many people would rather visit a webpage than read a long-winded resume or cover letter. Many people, including potential spouses, will turn immediately to your site to learn about you.

There are numerous apps that allow you to frame and manipulate multimedia materials in a creative and individualistic manner. In an Internet universe, where any piece of music can be paired with any photo and both can be manipulated to achieve virtually any end, investing some creative energy in a website has a huge payoff.

Professor Klassen, who is not quite as old as Professor Dwyer, has just learned how to create websites. His personal site is at www.thomasklassen.net. What choices has he made in building this page? Which of the four essential skills of professionals (communication, problem solving, teamwork, and adapting to change) has he highlighted? How does this site differ from his professional website at klassen.blog.yorku.ca?

When branding yourself, be aware of the way in which others might interpret you. Too many websites are egoistic exercises in self-discovery and self-promotion (the least effective kind of marketing).

It is fine to show people who you are and what you like. But Internet communication should always reflect the relationship-building function. This suggestion is in keeping with the recognition that a webpage or any on-line presence is unavoidably public. Although you don't need to eliminate all aspects of the private and the personal – after all, they make you unique and interesting – you should manage the difference between the public and the private to your best advantage.

If establishing your own webpage seems too daunting, join LinkedIn and create a profile there (see www.linkedin.com). LinkedIn is a social networking service, used mostly by professionals. It is an excellent way to contact others who share your educational and career interests, and to distribute your resume. We suggest that any student in his or her last year of studies (or even earlier) should join LinkedIn.

However, remember that your LinkedIn profile is available to everyone. Be sure that it perfectly matches your resume and transcripts.

More and more employers actively investigate the on-line presence of potential employees, looking for character defects and deficiencies that they will invariably inflate. Why? Because a difficult, renegade, or disaffected employee is a huge problem for an organization. Many individuals who unwisely see their professional identity as unaffected by their virtual identity have a rude awakening when they discover the lack of separation.

Internet dating as metaphor

This book relies heavily on the dating metaphor in illustrating the need for a good match between you and your courses, and then later between you and your employment position. We suggest that finding the right program of studies and the right job is a lot like dating. Dating denotes especially serious relationship building.

We argue that most of us take the search for a life partner very seriously and that we should take the same care in pursuing post-university employment.

In using the dating metaphor, we presumed two things. First, you would make an emotional connection between dating and job hunting that underlines important and often overlooked elements of the latter. Second, you already have a much deeper understanding of dating than you do of job hunting.

Our primary aim is not to endorse Internet dating, which might or might not work out in individual cases, but to suggest that serious relationship building must take the on-line environment into account. Moreover, we cite the case of Internet dating to illuminate what to embrace and what to avoid in all relationships that have an on-line component (it's increasingly difficult to imagine one that doesn't).

To find somebody to love, you must send out signals about yourself and your availability. For your parents and grandparents, this occurred during face-to-face contacts within families and religious groups, and perhaps at school or work.

Today more and more people are finding the "love of their lives" on-line or on Internet dating sites that require detailed information sharing. Engaging in Internet dating entails communicating who you are, not only with integrity, but also with critical and creative intelligence. Moreover, you are responsible for sifting through the signs and signals of others. A simple strategy for achieving this is to follow the example of employers – eliminate those who don't fit the blueprint or who send messages of instability, insecurity, unreliability, or any other undesirable trait.

When looking for employment, sending out signals is equally important. As outlined in the previous chapter, this is done via networking, but also increasingly also via your on-line presence, such as through LinkedIn, and your own website.

Internet dating could and should be a metaphor for all important relationship building in the modern age. It encapsulates the challenge that individuals face in their search for a personal space and deep relationships in a world where signs and signals proliferate but are often misleading. To think that critical and creative skills apply only in school or on the job is to ignore the really big work in our lives – finding and giving love. Critical and creative skills are impoverished unless we appreciate how they relate to the big themes of life.

Our most important relationships, apart from those with our parents, are with the people whom we choose to love. The love relationship is both an ideal template for all other significant relationships and the nurturing environment in which we develop ourselves. Finding a similarly positive environment at work will virtually guarantee a fulfilling and joyous life.

CHAPTER 11
Success at Work and Beyond

What is the recipe for successful achievement? To my mind there are just four essential ingredients: Choose a career you love, give it the best there is in you, seize your opportunities, and be a member of the team.

— Benjamin F. Fairless

You've landed your first job after graduation. Congratulations!

For a few weeks or months, you may feel much as you did during your first year of university. This will be a time of transition and new expectations. Virtually everything will be unfamiliar, and you'll need to figure it out quickly. Fortunately, your university years will have prepared you to absorb lots of information and make sense of it, and hopefully also provided you with the skills to add your own unique contribution.

At first, you may be somewhat disappointed by your job. It may have sounded exciting in the interview, but as you settle into it, you begin to realize that you are starting at the bottom. Your customers, students, clients, shifts, projects, and assignments are the dregs, allocated to you because no one else wanted them.

And that's no accident. Just before you arrived on the scene, your co-workers scooped up the cream. Don't despair. You were hired specifically because no one was available or willing to do these less appealing tasks. But now that you've got your foot in the door, it's time to demonstrate that you can learn rapidly and contribute, while graciously accepting that you're the new kid on the block.

The first job

During your first job, your colleagues and superiors will be closely assessing your personality. By showing that you are a contributor rather than a whiner at this difficult time, you can leave an indelible impression on them, one that will serve you well when opportunities arise for advancement.

New employees often desire to move ahead quickly. If you think that after two weeks, or two months, on the job, you've discovered a great new way of doing things that has never been considered before, think again. It's highly unlikely that you'll solve a long-standing problem in such a short time.

Presuming that you know best is also insulting and irritating to your colleagues and superiors. You will get a reputation for cockiness, and you certainly won't be seen as a team player. If only to demonstrate courtesy and respect, it is important to proceed cautiously at this stage.

At the same time, don't discount your observations either. By being new – and bringing to bear your university knowledge and expertise – you do have a contribution to make. In fact, your newness is a real advantage because it allows you to look at patterns and processes with fresh eyes.

Keep a diary or notes during the first few weeks, because once you have been at an organization for a while, you tend to accept things as they are. Everyone has a natural inclination to slide into routine and to become less able to question taken-for-granted assumptions. You may feel this tendency all the more because you desperately want to establish a comfort zone for yourself in your new position.

If you eventually want to make a positive contribution – particularly by thinking critically, or outside the box – it is crucial that you strive to maintain that sense of newness, curiosity, and questioning as long as possible. When you combine it with a bit more experience, you will add value to any organization.

As well, begin to specialize at work. Become more proficient than others in executing certain basic tasks. These may be the unexciting chores that everyone avoids, but mastering some of them is a very good idea because it allows you to add immediate value, enables you to really understand the business or process, and indicates the kind of person and employee that you will become.

Corporate recruiters frequently complain that many university graduates lack collaborative skills. Therefore, demonstrating that you are a team player will make a good impression. If you learned how to work in groups at university, this will pay dividends now.

If you are a team player, you may want to immediately be included in projects. The danger here is looking too pushy and aggressive. Be patient. Your superiors and colleagues will undoubtedly *feel you out* as a person and assess your talents before including you. Don't worry; they'll discover your potential soon enough! When this happens, you may find yourself besieged by requests for assistance.

Large and complex organizations commonly divide work into projects, and employees usually undertake a number of them simultaneously. As a result, they play many different roles. Your university experience of role playing in groups will help you here.

Also, depending on the number of projects in which you are involved, you may have numerous supervisors or colleagues. They may not be aware that you're working on multiple projects. Even if they are, it is human nature for managers to believe that their project is the most important and that their timetable and deadline are the only ones that count!

Fortunately, you have lots of related experience dealing with university professors, who all seem to set their assignment due dates in the same week. You've learned a lot about managing your time and working backward from deadlines. Hopefully, you've also learned that some tasks are more difficult than others and that some jobs and professors/employers are more demanding than others.

Trust yourself to make the necessary adjustments. Aim for competence and even excellence. But don't expect perfection. Nobody's perfect, but many people have burned themselves out by trying to be!

As you learn on the job, use the skills that you developed at university. Create a schedule, just as you did at school. Prioritize your tasks, and provide something extra via your research or the way in which you complete projects. Use your critical skills to identify what is most essential. Above all, show initiative and take criticism well. Much of your success at work will depend on how well you used your university time to learn, and hone, your skills.

Instead of being a stressful adjustment, your first weeks or months on the job might just be fun filled and exciting. Hey, you're making money. Unlike in school, you may have your weekends free. And term papers and essays are a thing of the past. As well, you're meeting new people and learning new skills and abilities.

Occasionally, a sense of excitement persists throughout a career. More commonly, however, it eventually wears off. After a few months or a year at work, many people become a little depressed. They're still at the same desk, in the same cubicle, doing the same tasks. Their work may not be fulfilling, and they're not even sure that it's being recognized. The daily grind of routine sets in, with a vacation break of just two weeks, instead of four months, on the distant horizon. Their initial excitement begins to dissipate, and they're dying for a change. Any change!

These feelings are natural. Unlike university instructors, managers rarely dole out grades or comments. They don't create transcripts that summarize what you learned or accomplished (job evaluations may take place only once a year). Instead of working with several teachers and many other students, you will typically have a smaller social group to stimulate you.

Many corporations and large organizations are hierarchical. You may feel that you are at the bottom of a very long ladder. Everyone else is above you, and your behaviour is constantly under scrutiny. Sure, at university, your professors had some power over you. But it was limited to one course, which you could always drop. And for every bad professor or teaching assistant, there was probably a good one who challenged or stimulated you.

Ironically, after four years of dreaming about graduating and getting out, you might actually find that you miss being a student. At least university offered something new and different at the start of each semester or term – new courses, new classmates, new professors, and new books.

If this occurs, remember that things are not as bad as they seem. Getting accustomed to the new rhythms of the workplace

may take a year or even two. But you'll gradually find that the rewards of a challenging and fulfilling job more than compensate for
the loss of your student life. Mastering tasks in the real world is
very satisfying. Moreover, you can always use your critical and creative skills to make your projects more gratifying.

Staying sharp

If you miss university, you can always take a course. If it relates to
your job, many employers will even pay part of your tuition. But
why not choose a subject that has nothing to do with work – one
that interests you? This is an excellent way to keep the creative
juices flowing.

To uncover exactly what you are missing, apply the problem-
solving skills from Chapter 7. If it turns out to be change, try to
find ways of varying your job. If it's self-development, use your
evenings and weekends to explore new interests. If you want to
develop more in-depth skills or insights, look for opportunities
to do this at work. You've become an expert at learning, so begin
to motivate and teach yourself inside and outside your job.

Most of all, don't limit your options. A broadly based university education, particularly in the liberal arts, provides you with
something that specialized or professional training can't deliver –
adaptability. Every employer is looking for staff who know how to
adapt, but you can also make it work for you.

The ultimate advantage of your university degree, with regard
to the job market, is flexibility. This provides the unparalleled capacity to pursue numerous options: self-employment, volunteering,
full- and part-time work, permanent and contract work, jobs in
other countries, and so many more.

Students often ask, "What the hell is a university degree good
for?" Answering this question is difficult because it's good for so
many things. University graduates work in all sorts of positions
that appear to have little relationship to their major or field of
studies.

Equally fascinating is how well they do in so many fields.
Their skills make them indispensable to their employers and allow them to move up the ladder reasonably quickly. But they also

have unequalled freedom to change jobs and even start their own businesses.

The freedom and flexibility, however, come with the responsibility to uncover their interests and to pursue them.

Dealing with the transition

The transition from school to work is not always smooth. Despite its stresses, students can become too comfortable in the university environment. By the time they graduate, they will have figured out how school works. And if they're good students, they may also be having a lot of fun.

At university, your work normally begins and ends within a few months, from the start of the semester to its conclusion. You advance in regular steps and get a degree in a relatively short time. At work, your career trajectory becomes far more elastic, with significant changes often taking much longer than you might expect.

It is an axiom that the workplace is characterized by change. But that won't necessarily apply to your personal advancement. Don't be too impatient. You will eventually find your comfort zone at work. The baby boomers are retiring, and you can look forward to considerably more opportunities for advancement in a few years. If you are just starting university now, your future prospects are particularly good.

If you are very unhappy or impatient at work, the job is probably not right for you, and you may need to think about moving on. Don't look on this change as something to be feared. Approach it as an opportunity for growth and renewed excitement.

After a few months or a year, you may decide that your job is not as rewarding as you'd expected. That's perfectly normal. After all, your first job is unlikely to match your ideal. Most people work two jobs during their first two years after graduation. The strategies and suggestions in this book can help as you search for the perfect fit between you and the requirements of a position.

Our advice about choosing your university courses applies equally well to deciding on a job. Follow what feels right. Consult your network and reflect on your interests, desires, and dreams. After a year or two in the workforce, you will not be the person you were in university. Below, we briefly discuss the strategies that any professional, at any stage of his or her career, needs to follow.

MOVING ON

Once you start working full-time, your resume becomes more important than ever. Update it every few weeks or months as you undertake new tasks and learn new skills. If you're continuing your education on a part-time basis, be sure to indicate this. You will be surprised by how often you're asked for your resume, sometimes on short notice.

Keep your list of references current as well. Your employer will be your key reference. For this reason, never burn your bridges at work, even if that means biting your tongue and swallowing your pride, difficult though it may be. Years later, you'll be glad you refrained from speaking your mind and may even recall difficult employers with fondness. In the same way, you may see your tough professors in a different light!

Once you've decided to move on, you need to do research. You will have developed your network while working and can start to touch base with key contacts. It is best to look for a job while still employed, so handing in your notice is usually not recommended until you have a firm offer.

Of course, that depends on the job you have. Some are so demanding in terms of time or pressure that you simply don't have the leisure to think, let alone engage in a job hunt. Some jobs don't provide you with the right contacts to build a decent network. These tend to be career dead ends. Bite the bullet: get out and begin a new job search.

If you do leave a position without a new one in hand, several months of hard work will probably elapse before you find a good job. Maintain your confidence during this time. When you doubt yourself, think of what you achieved by completing a university degree. If you could do that, you can do anything.

Try to avoid brooding on your situation. You won't feel unemployed if you treat your job search as full-time work. Get up early each day, dress as if you were going to the office, build your network, attend information interviews, rethink your career path, and assess your options. Looking for a job is the hardest job you'll ever have. If you do it well, you won't have time to get depressed and you'll eventually be successful.

A key ingredient for success, one that we've mentioned too briefly in this book, is confidence. Success at school gives one kind of confidence; succeeding at work instills another.

Being unemployed and looking for work tend to have a negative impact on confidence, which is why we recommend looking for a new job while you're still employed. But if you do find yourself without a job, you can always draw on one special kind of emotional currency – the self-esteem that arises from overcoming obstacles and completing a university degree.

You can also use your research and reading skills to cope with negative periods in your life and to develop the personal skills that will increase your chances of success. Although anxiety and depression are rife in the world, an abundant literature is available on how to become a happier, more confident person.

LEARNING DOES NOT END WITH A JOB

Be aware that your learning will not end once you start work. For an example, just consider that many people in senior professional positions used slide rules when they were in high school. They were never exposed to computers until well into their careers. Think of the learning they had to do. You will be faced with similar challenges as technology, laws, and professional and technological standards change during your career.

Fluidity and flexibility are bywords in the global marketplace. In a world characterized by constant change, the skill set developed at university is more relevant than ever before. But it is up to you – not your parents, your professors, or your employers – to make it alive and applicable in the present.

Graduate, professional, vocational, and on-line education

After a year or more in the labour force, you'll probably have a more precise image of the ideal job. At this point, you may decide to go back to school and further your education. Many professional and graduate schools look favourably on applicants who chose to work full-time after earning their bachelor's degree. In some MBA programs, working full-time for several years is an entrance requirement. Be sure to use your employment experience to advantage.

Graduate and professional schools are most concerned about accepting individuals who will complete their course of studies and then contribute to the profession. Applying to these schools is similar to applying for a job. Like employers, they want to avoid students who will become problems because they don't fit or cannot follow the rules.

The overriding focus of graduate and professional schools is not the intelligence or the academic potential of applicants. Rather, it is whether applicants have *what it takes* to finish the program and eventually become good colleagues in the profession.

In your application materials, demonstrate that you have carefully considered how you can (or wish to) contribute to your desired profession. Use your network to provide references that will support your statements. Be tenacious, even if you don't succeed the first time, or look for another way of reaching your goal, such as part-time or on-line studies. Few destinations can be approached via just one route.

If your undergraduate grades are not particularly high, explain why this is the case. Then supply evidence that both your capacity to learn and your motivation have improved since your undergraduate days. Achieving a few good grades in part-time courses will be useful here.

Your academic transcripts won't fully reflect your skills and abilities, but volunteer work can help fill this gap. In some professions, such as education and business, volunteer activities are weighted almost as heavily as academic scores.

Applicants to some graduate and professional programs are required to pass standardized exams, such as the LSAT or the GMAT. The key to acing these tests is familiarizing yourself with the questions they ask. There are thousands of Internet sites that provide questions for practice. You can find these by searching for "GMAT/ LSAT sample questions." In addition, many specialized books contain sample questions and strategies. Refer also to the section of multiple-choice tests in Chapter 3 of this book. People who work through many sample questions score significantly higher on standardized tests than those who don't.

You will need letters of reference for your application to graduate or professional schools, some of which will come from your professors. If you're wise, you will have kept in touch with one or two of them.

To ask for a letter of reference for a graduate application (or for a job), you need to take the following steps:

▸ Provide details about where you are applying and why.

▸ Ask the person if he or she can write you a "strong letter of reference." If the answer is "I'm not sure," or "Let me think about it," then politely explain that you will ask someone else. When requesting a letter you need to be proactive and ensure that the writer will portray you in the best possible light. For any number of reasons, some potential writers may not be able to do so. If that happens, find someone else.

▸ Send a copy of your transcript, or a list of courses and grades, to those who will be writing letters for you. Highlight the relevant courses and grades, especially those you have taken with the person writing the letter of reference. You can also list the papers that you wrote for the professor.

▸ Enclose your resume. The more information a professor has about you, the more helpful his or her letter will be. If your grades have recently improved or you have other relevant accomplishments, make a note of this. Highlight any accomplishment related to school or otherwise.

▸ Add your draft statement of interest. This will help your professor understand both your long-term objectives and why you are applying to the program.

▸ Explain how to submit the letter or reference (on-line or hard copy), and be sure to mention the deadline.

Following the above, and providing at least four weeks' advance notice, means that you will get the best possible reference, often praising your organizational skills. A rushed request with missing information results in a rushed letter with missing information –

and little chance of being accepted into the program. Follow up a week before the deadline with a gentle reminder.

The key component of a graduate school application is the statement of interest, which is much like the cover letter in a job application. It must be forward-looking: those who read it want to know what you will accomplish in the future – as a graduate student and then as a professional. They are not much interested in the past.

The statement of interest is not an autobiography or a justification of your undergraduate grades. Rather, it is a summary of what you intend to achieve as a graduate student: what topic or question you will explore and how you plan to undertake the exploration. You can also mention what scholarly influences have affected your decision to apply to the program: a particular book, or author, or theory. The statement of interest is an essay. Approach it as such.

Applying for graduate or professional school is considerable work, and it entails much research. The deadline for applications is sometimes almost a year in advance of the start of the program. You need to have a clear idea of what research or program you wish to pursue. A hurried application, like a sloppy resume, is a complete waste of time. Trust us on this one; we have a lot of experience.

COMMUNITY COLLEGE EDUCATION AND ON-LINE EDUCATION

In some instances, a college diploma or certificate can complement a university degree in achieving workplace success. The combination of university and college courses is becoming more common than in the past.

Again, there is research involved, including consulting your network about whether this option is right for you. Generally, a community college diploma is a good route if you have little work experience and/or you know exactly what type of job you wish to obtain.

The availability of on-line courses and programs, often part-time, opens up another route for post-undergraduate studies. At work, you'll sometimes need to learn a skill set or specific expertise that you don't possess. An on-line program might just be the best way of doing this.

The range of courses is astounding, from how to negotiate, to songwriting, to world history, taught by experts from around the world. Some are available at no cost and at whatever time and place are most convenient for you.[12]

Most undergraduate students find web-based courses demanding because they require considerable motivation. However, those with the right incentives, and with the listening, reading, and writing skills outlined in this book, usually flourish in on-line courses.

Further success

The road to the great job is just that, a road. You may reach your ideal job, only to discover that it is less so. Sometimes life is like that. The words of those aging rockers, the Rolling Stones, should be taken to heart: "You can't always get what you want. But if you try sometimes, you just might find, you get what you need."

You will encounter difficulties on the road, some possibly based on your gender, ethnic background, or personality. Again, the key is to trust your feelings and nourish your dreams. If a work situation or experience does not feel right, it's probably because your expertise and interests don't match the requirements of the position.

As you progress in the world of work, you will gain more experience (especially in trusting your feelings!) and will acquire reliable colleagues and associates who will advise you. The support of your network will be critical to your success and happiness. One or more of your professors may well belong to it, as will some of your friends from university.

Regardless of where your path may lead, the advantages and skills that you acquired at university will always be pertinent: communication, problem solving, teamwork, and adaptability. Use these well and your ultimate success is assured.

NOTES

1 Statistics Canada, "University Tuition Fees, 2014/2015," *The Daily*, 11 September 2014, http://www.statcan.gc.ca/daily-quotidien/140911/dq140911b-eng.htm.

2 As reported by Statistics Canada, *National Graduates Survey, 2013*, for 2009-10 graduates. For a summary, see Josh Dehaas, "National Graduates Survey Shows Class of 2010 Did Well," *Maclean's*, 8 April 2014, http://www.macleans.ca/work/jobs/national-graduate-survey-shows-class-of-2009-10-did-well/.

3 See Fox News, "Students' Use of Laptops in Class Lowers Grades: Canadian Study," 16 August 2013, http://www.youtube.com/watch?v=O2aybVf5QAM. The findings are reported in Faria Sana, Tina Weston, and Nicholas J. Cepeda, "Laptop Multitasking Hinders Classroom Learning for Both Users and Nearby Peers," *Computers and Education* 62 (March 2013): 24-31, http://www.sciencedirect.com/science/article/pii/S0360131512002254.

4 Adapted and used with permission from York University, Learning Skills Services.

5 The seven points are adapted from T.G. Gebremedhin and L.G. Tweeten, *Research Methods and Communication in the Social Sciences* (Westport, CT: Praeger, 1994), 92ff.

6 Michael Gilbert, *How to Win an Argument* (New York: John Wiley, 1996), 52.

7 Benjamin Bloom, *Taxonomy of Educational Objectives: Cognitive and Affective Domains* (New York: David McKay, 1956).

8 Donald A. Norman, *Things That Make Us Smart: Defending Human Attributes in the Age of the Machine* (New York: Addison-Wesley, 1993), 17.

9 Ulrich Kraft, "Unleashing Creativity," *Scientific American Mind* 16, 1 (April 2005): 16-23.
10 See Government of Canada, Services for Youth, "The Hidden Job Market," 22 May 2014, http://www.youth.gc.ca/eng/topics/jobs/looking.shtml.
11 Right Management Manpower Group, "Networking, Not Internet Cruising, Still Lands Most Jobs," press release, Toronto, 9 August 2012, http://www.rightmanagement.ca/en/news-and-events/press-releases/2012-press-releases/item23659.aspx.
12 For a place to start, visit Coursera, "Courses," 2014, http://www.coursera.org/courses, and Class Central, "Free Online Education," 2011-14, http://www.class-central.com.

MORE RESOURCES

Books

Babcock, L., and S. Laschever. (2009). *Ask for It: How Women Can Use the Power of Negotiation to Get What They Really Want*. New York: Random House.

Bailey, S. (2011). *Academic Writing for International Students of Business*. New York: Routledge.

Bain, K. (2012). *What the Best College Students Do*. Cambridge, MA: Harvard University Press.

Bolles, R.N. (2014). *What Color Is Your Parachute? 2015: A Practical Manual for Job-Hunters and Career-Changers*. Berkeley: Ten Speed Press.

Bowell, T., and G. Kemp. (2010). *Critical Thinking: A Concise Guide*. New York: Routledge.

Burke, D., and J. Pieterick. (2010). *Giving Students Effective Written Feedback*. Maidenhead, UK: McGraw-Hill Education.

Chiagouris, L. (2011). *The Secret to Getting a Job after College: Marketing Tactics to Turn Degrees into Dollars*. New York: Brand New World.

Cioffi, F.L. (2005). *The Imaginative Argument: A Practical Manifesto for Writers*. Princeton: Princeton University Press.

Cottrell, S. (2011). *Critical Thinking Skills: Developing Effective Analysis and Argument*. New York: Palgrave Macmillan.

Fitzpatrick, M. (2011). *Engaging Writing 2: Essential Skills for Academic Writing*. New York: Pearson Education.

Gilbert, M. (1996). *How to Win an Argument*. New York: John Wiley.

Gill, C.M. (2014). *Essential Writing Skills for College and Beyond*. Blue Ash, OH: Writer's Digest Books.

Gillett, A., A. Hammond, and M. Martala. (2009). *Inside Track to Successful Academic Writing*. Harlow, UK: Pearson Education.

Harvard University Business School. (2007). *Giving Presentations: Expert Solutions to Everyday Challenges*. Boston: Harvard Business School Press.

Hewings, M. (2005). *Advanced Grammar in Use*. Cambridge: Cambridge University Press.

Lispon, C. (2004). *Doing Honest Work in College: How to Prepare Citations, Avoid Plagiarism, and Achieve Real Academic Success*. Chicago: University of Chicago Press.

McMillan, K., and J. Weyers. (2010). *How to Write Essays and Assignments*. Harlow, UK: Pearson Education.

Messenger, W., J. de Bruyn, J. Brown, and R. Montagnes. (2014). *The Canadian Writer's Handbook*. Don Mills, ON: Oxford University Press.

Murphy, R. (2004). *English Grammar in Use*. Cambridge: Cambridge University Press.

Newport, C. (2007). *How to Become a Straight-A Student: The Unconventional Strategies Real College Students Use to Score High While Studying Less*. New York: Broadway.

Northey, M., and J. McKibbin. (2012). *Making Sense: A Student's Guide to Research and Writing*. Don Mills, ON: Oxford University Press.

Northey, M., L. Tepperman, and P. Albanese. (2012). *Making Sense in the Social Sciences: A Student's Guide to Research and Writing*. Don Mills, ON: Oxford University Press.

Oshima, A., and A. Hogue. (2006). *Writing Academic English: Level 4*. White Plains, NY: Pearson/Longman.

Pollak, L. (2012). *Getting from College to Career: Your Essential Guide to Succeeding in the Real World*. New York: Harper.

Powers, P. (2005). *Winning Job Interviews*. Franklin Lakes, NJ: Career Press.

Reinders, H., N. Moore, and M. Lewis. (2008). *The International Student Handbook*. London: Palgrave Macmillan.

Reynolds, G. (2012). *Presentation Zen: Simple Ideas on Presentation Design and Delivery*. Berkeley: New Riders.

Ruggerio, V.R. (1996). *Becoming a Critical Thinker*. Boston: Houghton-Mifflin.

Runion, M. (2004). *How to Use Power Phrases to Say What You Mean, Mean What You Say, and Get What You Want*. New York: McGraw-Hill.

Schultze, Q.J. (2012). *Resume 101: A Student and Recent-Grad Guide to Crafting Resumes and Cover Letters That Land Jobs*. New York: Ten Speed Press.

Shea, V., and W. Whitla. (2001). *Foundations: Critical Thinking, Reading and Writing*. Toronto: Pearson.

Swales, J.M., and C.B. Feak. (2007). *Academic Writing for Graduate Students*. Ann Arbor: University of Michigan Press.

Swan, M. (2005). *Practical English Usage*. Oxford: Oxford University Press.

Tissington, P., M. Hasel, and J. Matthiesen. (2009). *How to Write Successful Business and Management Essays*. Los Angeles: Sage.

Westerfield, J. (2002). *I Have to Give a Presentation, Now What?!* New York: Silver Lining Books.

Yate, M. (2004). *Resumes That Knock 'em Dead*. Avon, MA: Adams Media.

University and college resources

All universities have resources and services to help students learn and succeed after graduation. Check your own university or college to see what it provides. Here are four additional starting places:

Cornell University – Learning Strategies Center: http://lsc.cornell.edu/Sidebars/Study_Skills_Resources/SKResources.html.

Kwantlen Polytechnic University – Essential Skills Resources: http://www.kpu.ca/learningcentres/resources

Stanford University – Resumes/CVs and Cover Letters: https://studentaffairs.stanford.edu/cdc/resumes.

Wilfrid Laurier University – Study Skills Webinars: http://www.wlu.ca/page.php?grp_id=1866&p=12593.

YouTube writing aids

"How to Write an Effective Essay": https://www.youtube.com/watch?v=nWqMQ26Gqi4.

"How to Write an Effective Essay: The Introduction": https://www.youtube.com/watch?v=IN6IOSMviS4.

"How to Write an Essay": https://www.youtube.com/watch?v=liyFKUFCQno.

Canadian websites with job listings and career tools for young people

British Columbia, WorkBC: http://www.workbc.ca/.

Canada, Job Bank: http://www.jobbank.gc.ca/.

Charity Village (for those who are interested in the non-profit sector): http://charityvillage.com/.

Ontario, Youth Employment Services: http://www.yes.on.ca.

Quebec, Emploi Québec: http://emploiquebec.gouv.qc.ca/index.php?id=54&L=1.

ABOUT THE AUTHORS

THOMAS R. KLASSEN is a professor in the Department of Political Science and the School of Public Policy and Administration at York University. He earned his PhD in sociology from the University of Toronto while working full-time as a policy advisor in government. He has taught at Ryerson and Trent Universities as well as in Germany and South Korea, teaching a variety of courses in sociology, labour studies, political science, and public administration, including a course in the iMBA program at the Schulich School of Business.

The author of several books on labour market policy, he is the editor of many other books, including *Casino State: Legalized Gambling in Canada*. His most recent book is *Retirement in Canada*. He often writes for the mass media, including the *Toronto Star*, *Globe and Mail*, and others.

Before becoming a professor, he worked for ten years as a policy advisor in both social and economic policy, and also spent a year working for an Ottawa consulting firm. In the past decade, he has been a consultant on workplace and labour market issues to community agencies, legal firms, provincial and federal governments, and international agencies.

As a person who stutters – and never asked a single question in class during his entire high school education – he has written on the experience of people with disabilities. He is currently part of a large multi-year international development project, funded by the Government of Canada, to provide better employment opportunities for people with disabilities in Bangladesh, India, and Nepal.

On many days, he can be heard muttering, "No one listens to me, no one listens to me. My eight-year-old twins don't listen, my students don't listen, and my wife doesn't listen." He continually repeats himself, which he attributes to being a teacher, a father of twins, and a person who stutters – and to the fact that no one listens.

Early in 2014, he and his family moved to South Korea for two years because his wife had been transferred there by her employer. His portion of this book was written in Seoul. Unable to speak Korean, he notices that people don't pay attention when he speaks.

He recently learned to design his own website, of which he is proud: www.thomasklassen.net.

Professor Klassen can be reached at tklassen@yorku.ca.

JOHN A. DWYER is a professor in the Department of Humanities at York University in Toronto. He obtained his doctorate in the history of ideas at the University of British Columbia and has taught at the University of British Columbia, Simon Fraser University, and North Island College on Vancouver Island. He has edited numerous collections, written many journal articles, and is the author of two books on the economist and philosopher Adam Smith and the Scottish Enlightenment of the eighteenth century. His *Business History: Canada in the Global Community* is used by business schools as a textbook.

In addition to being a professor, he worked for many years as an administrator and consultant. He was acting director of placement for a major business school, where he helped broker matches between graduates and companies. He also worked as a frontier educator, a university fundraiser, a professional career developer, and as the associate director of a university teaching centre. As president of his own business, he provided consulting services to universities and colleges.

A gifted teacher and winner of many awards for his classroom activities, he has taught nearly everything, from natural science to history, ethics, and business. For several years, he taught a large undergraduate course on critical and analytical thinking for business at the Schulich School of Business. Most recently, he taught a course titled "On Love."

A rock music fan, his much-loved musicians include Joy Division, Radiohead, Sigur Rós, Pearl Jam, Nirvana, Dead Can Dance, Peter Gabriel, Björk, Richard Thompson, and especially, Pere Ubu. More esoteric preferences include Art Bears, Soft Machine, After Dinner, and Honeymoon Killers. His favourite food is "as exotic and spicy as I can get it – just as long as it's not fish." He hates fish, despite all attempts by his girlfriend (as she likes to be called) to hide it in stews and casseroles. But what he really fancies is expensive wine, brandy, and malt whiskies. He will drink beer, however, if there is nothing else.

When this book is published, he will be near retirement age. As a former hippie child of the sixties, he can even remember some things about the psychedelic period. He's still bitter about the era's false advertising with respect to "free love." He has an adult daughter from a previous marriage so likes to pretend that he understands young people.

Professor Dwyer can be reached at jdwyer@yorku.ca.